Aesthetic Life and Why It Matters

THINKING ART

Series Editors
Noël Carroll and Jesse Prinz, CUNY Graduate Center

Thinking Art fills an important gap in contemporary philosophy of art, focusing on cutting-edge ideas and approaches to the subject.

Published in the Series:

Aesthetic Life and Why It Matters

DOMINIC MCIVER LOPES, BENCE NANAY,
AND NICK RIGGLE

OXFORD
UNIVERSITY PRESS

OXFORD
UNIVERSITY PRESS

Oxford University Press is a department of the University of Oxford. It furthers the University's objective of excellence in research, scholarship, and education by publishing worldwide. Oxford is a registered trade mark of Oxford University Press in the UK and certain other countries.

Published in the United States of America by Oxford University Press
198 Madison Avenue, New York, NY 10016, United States of America.

© Oxford University Press 2022

First issued as an Oxford University Press paperback, 2023

Library of Congress Cataloging-in-Publication Data
Names: Lopes, Dominic, author. | Nanay, Bence, author. | Riggle, Nick, author.
Title: Aesthetic life and why it matters / Dominic McIver Lopes,
Bence Nanay, and Nick Riggle.
Description: New York, NY, United States of America :
Oxford University Press, [2022] | Series: Thinking art series |
Includes bibliographical references and index.
Identifiers: LCCN 2021038499 (print) | LCCN 2021038500 (ebook) |
ISBN 978-0-19-762579-8 (hbk) | ISBN 978-0-19-774851-0 (pbk) |
ISBN 978-0-19-762581-1 (epub)
Subjects: LCSH: Aesthetics. | Life.
Classification: LCC BH39 .L5959 2022 (print) | LCC BH39 (ebook) |
DDC 111/.85—dc23
LC record available at https://lccn.loc.gov/2021038499
LC ebook record available at https://lccn.loc.gov/2021038500

DOI: 10.1093/oso/9780197625798.001.0001

Paperback printed by Integrated Books International, United States of America

To our teachers, John Campbell, Rob Hopkins, David Velleman, and Richard Wollheim

Acknowledgments

For their generous and helpful comments, our thanks to the anonymous referees, Mary Beth Willard, Jonathan Gingerich, and an audience at the American Society for Aesthetics online festival during the summer of 2020.

Contents

Note for Instructors

Students seeking some introductory philosophy are almost always served a helping of value theory in the form of ethics. Some will have confronted serious moral dilemmas, and some are politically active: their experiences can be used to leverage philosophical reflection. Meanwhile, almost everyone is engaged in aesthetic life. Through encounters with peers, travel, and exposure to college town culture (and through the curriculum, too), universities and colleges intensify students' aesthetic lives and foment a fast-paced process of aesthetic discovery. For this reason, aesthetics is an ideal entry point to value theory, hence to philosophy. It invites and structures reflection on something that matters to most philosophy newcomers, at a time when its mattering is especially conspicuous to them. This volume is therefore an aesthetics appetizer, crafted to give a taste of philosophy at its best, as a tool for making sense of what we care about.

Each of the three contributors first offers an account of aesthetic life, or the modes of engagement and activity that go into it, and then makes a proposal about what aesthetic engagement contributes to a life that goes well. Bence Nanay sees aesthetic life as promoting achievement in having experiences. For Nick Riggle, aesthetic life is organized into social practices that foster communities of individuals, where neither community nor individuality must sacrifice to the other. Dominic McIver Lopes submits that the pluralism of aesthetic value practices answers to a human interest in exploring benign value differences. Yet more briefly, the three approaches emphasize *achievement, community*, and *diversity*.

All three proposals are original, building upon but neither repeating nor merely summarizing previous work by the three authors—which is cited in the Notes and Further Reading section that ends each chapter. Those who wish to enrich their understanding of the three proposals, or dissect their assumptions, have sources to consult. At the same time, each proposal is self-contained, can be read at one sitting, and has been written with beginning philosophers in mind.

The Introduction articulates three points of common ground that also open the volume up to its target audience. First, aesthetic engagement isn't limited to engagement with the fine arts. The tone throughout is radically ecumenical. Examples are drawn from outside the box of the traditional "fine arts"; they include food, fashion, video games, and hip-hop. Instructors unfamiliar with the philosophy of art need not fear that they will have to allay art anxiety fueled by elite culture. The ecumenical strategy also brackets intricate philosophical work on such topics as the nature and ontology of art, theories of artistic value, and theories of interpretation, metaphor, fiction, and depiction. Topics such as these are better left for specialized courses in aesthetics.

Second, all three proposals are set up as partial answers to what Bernard Williams, in *Ethics and the Limits of Philosophy*, called "Socrates's Question." The question is something like, how should one live? or what makes a life go well? It can also be a question about the meaningful life. For Williams, Socrates is not asking about moral demands, or even virtues. He is asking about all the ingredients of well-being. Applied to aesthetics, Socrates's question is about how aesthetic engagement spices up our lives. The book nicely complements discussions of the meaning of life, the good life, and well-being.

Finally, the Introduction explains how this book progresses beyond traditional thinking about aesthetic value. According to the traditional view, which has come to be called "aesthetic hedonism," an item's aesthetic value is its meriting pleasure, or its having the power to produce pleasure in suitably prepared responders. Plato held this view (in *Greater Hippias* 298a), as did most early moderns writing in aesthetics. Twentieth-century references include G. E. Moore in *Principia Ethica* and C. I. Lewis in his 1946 *Analysis of Knowledge and Valuation*. By the 1980s, aesthetic hedonism had become the default view, accepted without argument. Yet there are plenty of reasons for skepticism, some of them echoing skepticism about hedonism in general, some specific to aesthetic hedonism (for references, see the Introduction's Notes and Further Reading). Rather than wade into the weeds, the Introduction constructs an aesthetic variant of Robert Nozick's Experience Machine to show that it's worth at least considering how aesthetic life amounts to more than the pursuit of pleasure. The achievement, community, and diversity proposals run from there.

While this volume is slim and self-contained, it treats a problem in aesthetics that touches upon other topics in philosophy, especially topics that are good for philosophy newcomers to tackle. What's more, Lopes's, Nanay's, and Riggle's arguments have several implications, many of which also touch on broader issues in philosophy. In standard philosophical writing, interesting implications of an argument should be acknowledged. To avoid complicating the main chapters and to help generate critical discussion, points about disagreement, subjectivism, ethnocentrism, fads and fashions, and ideology critique are taken up in a Breakout discussion. The Breakout is also designed to model for students how to engage in constructive classroom dialogue focused on readings.

Teaching Connections

Some of the specific ideas developed in the three main chapters of this book suggest points of connection to topics that are commonly taught in introductory philosophy courses. The notes that follow are resources for those seeking either to integrate the material in this book into an existing course or to use the book to help conceive a new course. Needless to say, a different set of connections will be evident to those who might wish to teach the book in a specialized aesthetics course.

Nanay—Unlocking Experience

The main claim is that aesthetic experience is active—we work hard at it. This connects to issues in the philosophy of perception about the nature of experience, whether it's a fully passive mental phenomenon or rather an active one.

Nanay's claim that aesthetic experience can be an achievement connects to work on emotion regulation. Emotions are very often regulated, and while down-regulating (suppressing anger or fear) has received more attention, up-regulating (trying to feel an emotion more intensely) is equally important. One question worth asking is how the idea of aesthetic experience as achievement relates to emotional up-regulating.

The argument that it's aesthetic experience and not aesthetic judgment that we care about presupposes a sharp distinction between judgment and experience. This echoes questions in philosophy of mind about the difference between perception and belief.

Can we fully know someone else's aesthetic experience? The question connects up nicely with issues addressed in Thomas Nagel's "What Is It Like to Be a Bat"; Frank Jackson's papers about Mary, the vision scientist; and Laurie Paul's work on transformative experiences.

Nanay argues that there are huge cross-cultural variations in aesthetic experience. This could lead into a discussion of cultural influences on perception and of linguistic determinants of perceptual processes.

Riggle—Aesthetic Lives: Individuality, Freedom, Community

A course with a unit on the ethics of killing animals for food can consider Riggle's theory of food in relation to how Peter Singer thinks of food in "All Animals Are Equal." The class might wonder more generally about what theories of food underlie debates about the ethics of eating.

A unit on metaphysics could introduce students to the concepts of natural kinds, social kinds, and functional kinds. Students can study Riggle's theory of aesthetic value as a detailed example of how social and functional kinds can interact.

Riggle argues that there's a tension between treating something as having aesthetic value and treating it as being food. This applies to discussions of cultural food appropriation, where food is mistreated as such. This can tie into discussions of respect for other cultures, cosmopolitanism, and free markets.

Students who're studying freedom in units on free will or political philosophy can compare the notions of freedom explored there to Riggle's notion of aesthetic freedom. How does aesthetic life fit (or not) with different political philosophies?

Courses that cover personal identity or the self can connect those discussions to the idea that we have an aesthetic self.

Lopes—Getting into It: Ventures in Aesthetic Life

If you teach Nozick's Experience Machine or Gettier cases, explore their similarity to the *Broadway Boogie Woogie* case. All are arguments that show how a phenomenon supervenes on more than appears.

Lopes defines social practices as patterns of behavior explained by norm compliance. Discuss what's meant by a norm. It can be interesting to make explicit tacit norms, such as norms for being a student or a teacher. Social media erode aesthetic life by trapping us in echo chambers. If you're doing some epistemology, a parallel point can be made about how echo chambers erode trust and testimonial justice. Students will have a vague concept of relativism. "Pluralist" value schemes have five specific traits. Focus on the five traits to articulate conceptions of relativism.

The chapter assumes that an aesthetic monoculture would be bad and that we have an interest in easy encounters with difference. Lopes also suggests that political philosophy overemphasizes conflicting values. An interesting connection is to Mill on experiments in living, in chapter three of *On Liberty*.

Aesthetic Life and Why It Matters

Introduction

1. Your Aesthetic Life

You have a complex and detailed aesthetic life.

You make aesthetic decisions every day. You wake up, shower, and dress. When you decide what to wear, you think about how it feels and fits, how it expresses your style. You wander into the kitchen and think about what to eat. When you decide what to eat, you think about flavor, texture, smell. You head out into the world. You see your car, your bike, your shoes and appreciate how they look. When you decide what to buy, you think about how it will look in your house, or how it sounds or feels. You make aesthetic decisions every day—about what to listen to, what to watch, whether to arrange things just so, about how to sit, strut, or sing.

You have aesthetic feelings and reactions every day. The sunset swings into view as you turn a corner and you think, "That's beautiful." A wave of calm and pleasure washes over you. You take a bite of cake and you think, "Wow, that's sweet. Maybe too sweet." You hear that new song and it blows you away. You play it on repeat and for your friends. You try the new restaurant and you think: "It's bland, boring, awesome, exciting, brilliant, bold." The novel is wonderful, the film disappoints, the dress looked better in the store. You have aesthetic feelings and reactions every day, and these reactions move you through the world and shape your sense of self and well-being.

You create aesthetic looks, atmospheres, and objects every day. When you dress, you create an outfit that you put into the world. When you have friends over, you play music, light a candle, arrange

Aesthetic Life and Why It Matters. Dominic McIver Lopes, Bence Nanay, and Nick Riggle, Oxford University Press. © Oxford University Press 2022. DOI: 10.1093/oso/9780197625798.003.0001

the dinner table, set a mood. You exercise aesthetic creativity when you design your tattoo, put on makeup, pierce your ear or nose, spritz cologne or perfume, or pay close attention to your hair. Almost everything you do has an aesthetic dimension—from the way you make your bed, prepare your coffee, and tie your shoes, to the way you speak to others and adjust photos to post on social media. You create aesthetic value every day.

You have a complex and detailed aesthetic life that you orchestrate every day through your aesthetic decisions, reactions, feelings, and actions. One reason you might think that you don't have an aesthetic life is that you think of "aesthetic" as "art." "I don't have an aesthetic life," you might think, "because I never go to the museums or galleries. I don't own any paintings or sculptures (and don't want to). I barely know anything about classical music, I've never been to an opera, and I've only been to two fancy restaurants. Aesthetic life is for art lovers, people who love the fine arts and 'high' culture."

This thought is understandable. A concern with the aesthetic is often depicted in films, literature, and TV as a concern with art and so-called high culture—we think of pristine white galleries and expensive paintings, people with highly refined and educated judgment, dramatic opera performances and tuxedos, red carpets and expensive dinners. We also tend to think that caring about aesthetic value is an exclusive privilege, only for people who are part of the "in" crowd, or who have money, or education, or a lot of time on their hands. We think of condescending snobs, cold critics, and self-absorbed, aloof artists.

But this way of thinking isn't right. For one thing, it confuses aesthetic life with a concern for so-called fine art. Your aesthetic life is your life of engaging with aesthetic value and disvalue. It's the life you live with things that you think are beautiful, ugly, cute, sleek, lovely, garish, awesome, amazing. You might not use those words. You might use other more inventive terms: dope, tight, fresh, wack, lit, sick, extra, or basic. We use these words to describe sneakers, outfits, apps, games, burritos, people, TV shows, coffee beans, and candy. And art. Some of the things in your aesthetic life are "art," but many of them are not.

Furthermore, we should not think of "art" as restricted to the traditional "fine arts": painting, sculpture, music, poetry, and architecture. Art also includes performance art, film, street art, conceptual art, dance, graffiti, literature, photography, land art, haute couture, culinary art, video art, and social practice. And you can live an aesthetic life—you can engage with aesthetic value—even if you don't engage with any of these arts.

And finally, a concern with aesthetic value is simply part of what it is to be alive, to be human. It's not only for an elite or exclusive club. It's for everyone. Morality isn't only for do-gooders. Justice isn't only for judges. We're all affected by aesthetic value; we all engage with it, we all create it—especially in the twenty-first century, in a world where almost everything we encounter is designed, considered, and shaped with aesthetic value in mind. Like morality and justice, your aesthetic life is an inescapable, sublime, profound, and mysterious part of life. The aesthetic world will transform and shape you, define your sense of community, structure the way you think, feel, create, and love. It already is, and will continue to be, woven into the very fabric of your self.

You have a complex, detailed, and important aesthetic life that you orchestrate every day. But what is aesthetic value? Why should you care about it? What is the point of living an aesthetic life at all? And how should you live your aesthetic life?

2. Socrates's Question of Aesthetics

In his masterpiece, *The Republic* (376 BCE), the ancient Greek philosopher Plato portrays his teacher Socrates conversing with friends and rivals about a fundamental question of philosophy: how should we live our lives? The fact that we're aware of how we have lives to lead means that we have to rise to the challenge of living them well. Let's mull the question over a bit and then turn to the more specific question about our aesthetic lives.

Notice that Socrates doesn't ask how we actually live our lives; he asks how we *should* live them. We sometimes feel that we're not measuring up. Someone thinks, "I worry a lot about how others see me. I should get over it." Or they think, "I don't really understand climate change. I should learn more." We constantly measure how we are against an image of how we should be. Doing this motivates us to act. We also have to make decisions about our future. If you're a student, the moment of peak life decisions is fast approaching. It's no time to put your aspirations on the back burner.

In the normal course of affairs, Socrates's question tends to arise in the guise of specific dilemmas. This school or that one? Is this person the one? Have a life or accept the job offer at the startup? Risk comfort and security or look the other way? Socrates obviously can't advise on specifics. Philosophy answers Socrates's question by listing the general kinds of ingredients that go into well-being. For example, Socrates himself thought that cultivating an active and self-reflective mind is part of the good life for anyone. That might be a general ingredient of well-being.

General answers to Socrates's question don't assume that everyone is the same. On the contrary, they're meant to accommodate individual and cultural differences. Suppose that having an active mind is part of the good life for anyone. That leaves it entirely open whether you're better off majoring in marketing or computer science. Likewise, listing aesthetic engagement among the ingredients of a good life doesn't dictate what you should be into, in particular. Artisanal pickling or baroque harpsichord? Both? Your aesthetic interests might express your individuality.

There are so many different kinds of value. All in one day, you're struck by the cleverness of a classmate's comment on the reading, you buy a six pack of snack ramen because it's a good deal, you toss around a Frisbee to unwind, you admire the solid construction of a leather purse at the fair trade shop, you envy the courage of some student activists. Smarts, good deals, relaxation, purses that don't let coins fall out, and courage are all good things that we should have in our lives.

Yet it's tempting to hear Socrates's question as a moral question. Heard morally, "How should we live our lives?" becomes "What are our moral obligations?" or "What is the moral ideal?" But this is an error. Socrates's question isn't just moral. It's tragic to make the wrong choice when the trolley is careening toward five innocents tied to the tracks, and you can save them only by diverting it onto a track where one innocent will die. But is it enough, when looking back on your existence, to have nothing better to say than "I did my duty"? You might fulfill your moral obligations, giving others exactly what you owe them, and still be left wondering what you should do about the nonmoral aspects of your life. Should you major in medieval studies? Should you marry? Should you take up scuba? These are fair questions, and morality can't answer them. In other words, your ideal life might not be to emulate a moral saint who's totally dedicated to others. For most of us, attending to moral obligations is an essential minimum to living well, but it's not the whole enchilada.

What might go into the enchilada, beyond getting a perfect moral report card? Some strong contenders include love and friendship, achievement, an absorbing career, opportunities to collaborate with others to advance the collective good, spiritual devotion, sensuous enjoyment, and intellectual thrills. Some of these might not work for you, and you might want to lengthen the list. For now, what about aesthetic engagement?

You, and the people around you, already lead rich aesthetic lives. Remember that aesthetic engagement isn't limited to the "fine arts." To live an aesthetic life, you don't have to ditch Super Mario for *La Traviata*. This fact, emphasized in the first section, contains two important lessons.

On one hand, a broad and welcoming picture of aesthetic life makes it easier to answer Socrates's question of aesthetics. Imagine an "anaesthete," a person who's utterly cold to everything aesthetic. They don't listen to music, only read for work, pay zero attention to how they dress and what they eat, don't have time for movies and TV, and see no point in a walk on the beach. The philosopher Mary Mothersill reckoned that only great trauma could entirely numb a human being to aesthetic value.

The lesson is that we mustn't set the bar too high as we try to make sense of the place of aesthetic engagement in our lives. There's no need to convince the anaesthete that they're missing something. They say, "I have no aesthetic life. So what?" Maybe there's an answer to them; maybe not. It doesn't matter. Most of us are already involved in the flow of aesthetic life and can't even remember a time when we weren't. We don't need to be convinced of what we'd be missing if some trauma wiped out our aesthetic capacities. We know that aesthetic engagement matters. The puzzle is why it matters.

On the other hand, the broad and welcoming picture of aesthetic life poses a challenge. Take a course in music appreciation, art history, literature, or film studies, and you'll learn a lot about the "classics," and also about artworks that promise a glimpse of overlooked perspectives. Works like these teach important truths. They motivate us to be our better selves. They're touchstones of cultural identity and memory.

The lesson is that, because they're important in these special ways, we can't focus only on them when we tackle Socrates's question of aesthetics. It would be a terrible mistake to regard a quirky style of dressing or a perfect poké as lesser counterparts of Margaret Atwood's *Handmaid's Tale*. Don't be tempted to reason like this: "Look, here's what we get from ballet and Atwood's novels. Fashion and poké are the same, only less good." An honest answer to Socrates's question of aesthetics should make sense of the life engaged with developing a quirky style of dress or hunting for the perfect poké in its own terms. We know that such a life does matter. The puzzle is why.

3. Why Do We Care?

Imagine a movie that's so fascinating, funny, and entertaining that if someone watches it, they just want to keep on watching it over and over again. They have no desire to watch anything else. In fact, they can't even tear their eyes from the screen in order to eat, and they die in a couple of days. The American writer David Foster Wallace wrote a very long, not particularly easy to read novel, called *Infinite Jest*, about such a movie. In the novel, only one copy of the movie exists, which is itself called *Infinite Jest*, and because of the deadly consequences of watching it, the film becomes a lethal weapon, coveted by various countries.

Would you watch the movie? Probably not, as you know that it would mean certain death in a couple of days. But let's modify the example a bit. The film is equally fascinating, funny, and entertaining, but you can tear yourself away to eat, sleep, do your daily work, and live the rest of your nonaesthetic life. The catch is that you'll never watch another movie or TV show, or read another novel, or listen to music. This nonlethal version of the movie, let's call it *Infinite Jest Lite*, gives you the maximal amount of aesthetic thrills you can possibly get.

Would you watch it in this modified scenario? We suspect that very few people would. But why not? Here are some options.

You fear that you're missing out on some other aesthetic thrills. But this can't be it. By definition, *Infinite Jest Lite* delivers the maximum you can ever expect from any aesthetic activity. So it's all the stuff you're afraid of missing out on, and more, wrapped into one single film. If you watch it, and keep on watching it over and over again, you won't miss out on any aesthetic kicks. This is a built-in feature of the example.

Maybe you think that watching the same movie over and over again would be boring. But that's not true in this particular case. By definition, the movie gets more and more enticing every time you watch it. Nonetheless, you wouldn't let yourself fall into the trap. Figuring out the source of this reluctance tells us a lot about the importance of aesthetics in our life.

The three very different approaches that this book presents share the assumption that you would miss out on something important if you watch *Infinite Jest Lite*. They assume there's more to aesthetic life than whatever watching the movie over and over could bring you. Something really important would be missing, and the three chapters give overlapping but different takes on what this amounts to.

Bence Nanay argues that we often experience aesthetic engagement as an achievement. What we really care about in aesthetic life is aesthetic experiences, and aesthetic experiences are often something we work hard to achieve. Part of the importance of aesthetic experiences comes from the sense of accomplishment. And when shared with others, our achievement gains further importance. All of this would be missing from the lives of those who opt to watch *Infinite Jest Lite* over and over again.

Nick Riggle develops the idea that aesthetic engagement allows us to cultivate our individuality—our sense of humor, our creative and expressive abilities, our taste in dress and design, our love of certain bands, writers, or cuisines. As aesthetically engaged individuals, we gain access to unique forms of community. We commune with those who love the same bands as us, whose style we find alluring, or whose unusual sensibility challenges us and inspires us to try new things. Aesthetic engagement offers unique ways of being and bonding that we cannot live without.

Dominic McIver Lopes sees aesthetic engagement as especially well suited to satisfy a hunger we have for difference. Most people like potato chips. According to statista.com, barbecue flavor is very popular, the preferred choice of eighty-five million customers in the United States alone. Yet many of these eighty-five million sometimes choose a different flavor. They're even willing to try experimental new flavors. Falafel flavor! Cantaloupe flavor! There would be something strange going on if they didn't. Human beings need to get out of their comfort zones. But why? Comfort zones are where the comfort is. Why ever leave them? Lopes explains why pure difference can make such a difference.

Notes and Further Reading

1. The sociologist Jennifer Lena tells the history of aesthetic elites in the United States in her book, *Entitled: Discriminating Tastes and the Expansion of the Arts* (Princeton University Press, 2019). On the aesthetic as the domain where things are cute, awesome, or garish, see Frank Sibley, "Aesthetic Concepts," *Philosophical Review* 68, no. 4 (1959): 421–450. A list of aesthetic concepts is at http://www.linguaaesthetica.com. On the nature of art, see Arthur C. Danto, "The Artworld," *Journal of Philosophy* 61, no. 19 (1964): 571–584 and Noël Carroll, "Art and Interaction," *Journal of Aesthetics and Art Criticism* 45, no. 1 (1986): 57–68. On the pervasiveness of the aesthetic, see Yuriko Saito, *Everyday Aesthetics* (Oxford University Press, 2007) and her useful encyclopedia article, "Aesthetics of the Everyday," *Stanford Encyclopedia of Philosophy* at https://plato.stanford.edu/entries/aesthetics-of-everyday/.

2. On Socrates's question, see Bernard Williams, *Ethics and the Limits of Philosophy* (Harvard University Press, 1985), 1–4. Another approach to Socrates's question focuses on the meaning of life. See Susan Wolf, *Meaning in Life and Why It Matters* (Princeton University Press, 2010). Susan Wolf rejects moral sainthood as the ideal for life in her paper, "Moral Saints," *Journal of Philosophy* 79, no. 8 (1982): 419–439. A compact and accessible inventory of answers to Socrates's question is in Thomas Hurka, *The Best Things in Life: A Guide to What Really Matters* (Oxford University Press, 2011). Mary Mothersill discusses anaesthetes in *Beauty Restored* (Oxford University Press, 1984).

3. The *Infinite Jest* story is similar to, and is likely to be inspired by, a thought experiment by the philosopher Robert Nozick involving an "Experience Machine" that gives you all the pleasures you can possibly have. Again, the question is: would you get in? Nozick suggests that people would not, and he uses these considerations to argue against hedonism, the view that pleasure is the only genuine value. Others argue that what's missing if you get in the Experience Machine is the sense of accomplishment or achievement; see

Thomas Hurka, *The Best Things in Life: A Guide to What Really Matters* (Oxford University Press, 2011). The Experience Machine thought experiment is in Robert Nozick, *Anarchy, State and Utopia* (Basic Books, 1974), 42–45. For the view that aesthetic life is the pursuit of pleasure, see Jerrold Levinson, "Hume's Standard of Taste: The Real Problem," *Journal of Aesthetics and Art Criticism* 60, no. 3 (2002): 227–238. An excellent summary of aesthetic hedonism is Servaas Van der Berg, "Aesthetic Hedonism and Its Critics," *Philosophy Compass* 15, no. 1 (2020): 1–15.

1

Unlocking Experience

Bence Nanay

1. Why Do We Care?

We spend a lot of money on aesthetic goods. Concert tickets, gourmet meals, fancy shoes, music and video streaming services, a night at the opera, a trip to see the Taj Mahal. In fact, I myself seem to spend most of my money on aesthetic goods. But even when we spend money on other things (buying a car, renovating our house, booking a hotel room), our decisions are to a large extent based on aesthetic considerations (about how the car looks, the color of the new wall paint, the view from the hotel room). Why do we care so much about these things that we spend all this money on them?

But it's not all about money. We also spend an amazing amount of time on aesthetic pursuits, from watching clips on YouTube to spending a day in the museum or reading a seven-volume novel of four thousand pages. Why do we do this to ourselves? But it's not only about time either.

We deeply care about aesthetic stuff in our personal life and relationships. It can be extremely disillusioning if your close friend has the opposite aesthetic reaction from yours. She hates the film you just watched together, and you loved it. There is something jarring when that happens. I'm not saying it's the end of the friendship, but it can be an alienating experience. And if you find out at your first date that your potential romantic partner likes very different music, films, and books, this often leads to no second date, even if the chemistry is there.

Aesthetic Life and Why It Matters. Dominic McIver Lopes, Bence Nanay, and Nick Riggle, Oxford University Press. © Oxford University Press 2022. DOI: 10.1093/oso/9780197625798.003.0002

Why do we care so much? Why do we seem to care about the aesthetic domain more than about pretty much any other domain? I don't think the second date would be in danger just because we disagreed about how we would solve some ethical dilemmas. And with the exception of maybe the most effective of effective altruists, most of us spend more money on aesthetic pursuits than on donations to charities. What makes aesthetics matter to us so much?

It should be clear that by "aesthetic" I don't mean high art. Going to the opera or to a museum exhibition is an aesthetic pursuit, but so is watching a sitcom or listening to hard house. And also going hiking in the autumn forest or choosing your outfit for the day. It's a mistake to assume that aesthetics is by definition elitist. In fact, in order to understand why it matters so much to all of us, we should just drop any elitist connotations of the concept. I'll go through five often voiced answers about why aesthetics matters before settling on a sixth, which is about aesthetic experiences.

1.1. First Answer: We Don't Actually Care

Someone might say that all this is misguided. Maybe some people, self-involved snobs, spend all their money on aesthetic stuff, but most people spend all their money on the absolute basics and also the most functional things they can get, irrespective of any aesthetic considerations. And our relationships are not based on insubstantial aesthetic agreements and disagreements but rather on political or ideological alignments.

I'm sure this is exactly what some people think of themselves, but I think they underestimate the reach of the aesthetic domain. We all need to eat and drink, and right there we face an aesthetic choice about how much aesthetic pleasure we expect to get out of, say, eating this kind of bread or that kind of bread or just how much salt we should put in the soup. Not just gourmet meals in

Michelin-starred restaurants count as aesthetic. Choosing straw-berry instead of vanilla at the ice cream stand is as much an aesthetic choice as choosing the eleven-course tasting menu instead of the nine-course one. And without discounting the importance of political and ideological alignments (especially in today's polarized political climate), I find it difficult to believe that anyone would seriously claim that this explains all our deepest relationships.

But don't take my word for it. The importance of aesthetic preferences for our lives can be examined experimentally. Imagine that you wake up tomorrow and you're suddenly a foot taller than you are now. Or shorter. Or blond and not brunette. Or smarter. Or less funny. Or a Democrat and not a Republican. Or have a very different musical taste. The question is: would this person still be you? And this is exactly the question that experimenters asked lots of people concerning many of these scenarios.

The results are somewhat surprising: physical changes don't seem to influence whether you think that this person would still be you. Nor do intellectual or even ideological changes. But aesthetic preferences do! If you are a fan of thrash metal and you need to imagine that tomorrow you wake up a Justin Bieber fan, you tend to feel that that person isn't you—it's someone else. We consider our musical preferences, like being a fan of thrash metal, to be a much more integral part of who we think we are than how smart or funny we are, or where our political allegiances lie. In short, aesthetics does matter and it matters a lot, even to those who try to deny this fact.

1.2. Second Answer: We Care about Entertainment, Not Aesthetics

The second strategy for downplaying the importance of aesthetics is to make a sharp distinction between "true aesthetics" and "mere entertainment." Yes, some people spend a lot of money on going to raves or hip-hop concerts, but there's nothing aesthetic about this; this is merely entertainment. Or some people may watch superhero movies, but this has nothing to do with aesthetics or even with "cinema," as the famed film director Martin Scorsese recently claimed.

Probably the most well-known advocate of drawing a strict line between art and the aesthetic domain, on one hand, and "mere entertainment," on the other, was the twentieth-century German sociologist and cultural theorist Theodor Adorno. Adorno's main interest was music. He was writing at a time when popular music was emerging as a genuine alternative to classical music, and he sought to defend the bastions of "real" music against these popular infiltrations.

But what counted as popular music at the time when Adorno was lashing out against it was the classic jazz orchestra, like Duke Ellington's. Even the snobbiest of snobs today would consider Duke Ellington to be as much part of most elite circle of high culture as anyone. The point is that any attempt at dividing up culture into high culture (which is the domain of aesthetics) and low culture (which is the domain of "mere entertainment") is just crazy, because these divisions (even if they exist) are very malleable.

Take film. Here, Adorno doesn't even distinguish between high and low forms of film, but just puts all films into the "mere entertainment" category, including films that are now widely considered to be the peak high art achievements of the first half of the twentieth century.

My aim is not to pick on Adorno. But many people share the same attitude today. To return to the controversial remark by Scorsese about Marvel movies, the film he explicitly criticized was *Avengers: Endgame*, which was directed by the Russo brothers, who also directed many episodes of probably the most deeply high-concept and most critically acclaimed sitcom of the last decade, NBC's *Community*. Further, some could also question the high culture credentials of the—let's face it—solidly middlebrow Scorsese. To make any attempted aesthetics/mere entertainment distinction even more complicated, many works explicitly aim to capture the most elitist audiences while at the same time catering to the widest popular taste. The musical *Hamilton* and the sitcom *Arrested Development* come to mind as examples.

In short, at no point in time can we rigidly separate high culture (aesthetics) and low culture (mere entertainment). But even if we could, these division lines change extremely rapidly over time. So it makes no sense to reserve the label of aesthetics, as a badge of honor to some select elitist pieces.

1.3. Third Answer: We Care Because We Want to Impress Others

Another influential line of reasoning is that we don't spend money on music, theater, films, and gourmet meals for aesthetic reasons. We do so in order to signal our social status or social aspirations. So when we go to the opera, we don't do this because we like listening to opera, but in order to be seen by others so that they know that we share their taste. And we listen to music not for the experience of listening to music but in order to signal our musical preferences to people around us. The subtext here is that we aspire to belong to a certain social class, and we signal the aesthetic taste of that social class.

I believe that this account is just factually incorrect, but if it were correct, it would paint an extremely depressing picture of humankind. Remember, the suggestion is that we signal the aesthetic taste we believe the social class we hope to belong to has. But this is true of everybody. So those people whom we are trying to impress with our musical taste try to impress us with their musical taste. So nobody actually likes the music they listen to—neither us nor them. We all just pretend to like it so that we will fit in with all these other people who also pretend in order to fit in. Not a very uplifting picture of what we spend much of our time and money on.

Luckily, it's very unlikely that this picture is even remotely correct. Suppose it's true that we go to a certain restaurant in order to be seen there by our neighbors and friends. Once there, you still need to choose what to order, and here genuine aesthetic preferences will kick in. Or you go to the museum to be seen there by other museum-goers. But which museum you go to, which wing of that museum, which room, or which painting you'll spend time looking at is still underspecified by any of the "impressing others" considerations.

A mild version of this "impressing others" approach is very likely to be true. There are some things of an aesthetic nature that we do in order to impress others. We choose the kind of wallpaper that featured in our favorite home decor magazine. We go and see a performance or a film because everybody is talking about it. And so on. But there's a difference between saying that some of our aesthetic choices take into consideration the social impact of our choices and saying that all of our aesthetic choices are determined by this. Even if some of our aesthetic choices take into consideration the social impact of our choices, there's plenty of room for genuine aesthetic considerations.

Further, many of our aesthetic activities are fully private. We read books before going to sleep in the solitude of our bedroom, we listen to music in our car when nobody else hears it, we watch TV series at work sneakily with the office door closed, and maybe even in private browsing mode. Who are we trying to impress then? This takes us to the fourth potential answer.

1.4. Fourth Answer: We Care Because We Want to Impress Ourselves

This is a version of the previous answer. But instead of trying to signal our aesthetic taste to others, it's ourselves whom we are trying to signal to. The general thought is that we would like to think of ourselves as sophisticated, cultured people, and we adopt our aesthetic tastes accordingly. This makes the last worry about the previous answer go away. When we listen to music in our car all alone, with the windows up, we're not trying to impress our neighbors or the random passerby. We're trying to impress ourselves. Or rather, we're trying to strengthen the self-image we have of ourselves.

And this move also solves the other problems about the previous answer: when I choose a painting to look at in the museum, even if I have already signaled that I'm a museum-goer, I'm doing this with an eye on what I think I should be doing, being the sophisticated art consumer I am. And I order the meal in the fancy restaurant that would fit best with my self-image as a huge foodie and Thai food connoisseur.

We certainly do this at least sometimes. But I don't think this explains why we care about aesthetics so strongly. And it can't account for the phenomenon often referred to as "guilty pleasures." We often like listening to music that's not very good, and we know it's not very good. We know that in some sense of "should" we should not be listening to it, but we do. That would be a guilty pleasure— guilty because we feel a shade of guilt that we are enjoying listening to it (although we shouldn't).

Confessional moment: while I'm incredibly snobby in my choice of films, and I watch almost exclusively 1960s modernist black-and-white Italian or French films where absolutely nothing happens, I do have a guilty pleasure: sitcoms. And not just the respectable ones, like *Seinfeld*, but also *Friends*, even *That 70s Show*. *That 70s Show* is not great from a cinematic point of view. It's no Antonioni. Not even consistently funny, if I want to be honest. It's also not exactly politically correct from today's point of view. But I do sometimes watch episodes of it; in fact, I watched quite a few during the 2020 lockdown. I could have been watching Godard or Kiarostami, but I chose to watch *That 70s Show*.

If all there was to aesthetic choice was the imperative to try to impress ourselves, then none of us would have guilty pleasures. But we all do. When you indulge in guilty pleasures, you're not just failing to impress yourself; you're acting against your aesthetic self-image (which is supposed to dictate what you do). The very existence of guilty pleasures shows that the "impressing ourselves" answer isn't the full answer.

I'm actually quite skeptical of the usefulness of the concept of guilty pleasures, because it embodies a form of normativity that we should all be very suspicious about. When I introduced the concept of guilty pleasures, I used the word "should" a lot: you're listening to music you don't think you *should* listen to. But where does this normativity come from? In some sense it comes from the normativity of taking your self-image too seriously. You think of yourself as a modernist 1960s black-and-white film guy, so the kind of films you "should" watch are modernist 1960s black-and-white films. Or you think of yourself as a huge foodie, so you "should" always eat sophisticated gourmet food. Under no circumstances should you eat at McDonalds, let alone enjoy it. If you do enjoy it, this counts as a guilty pleasure.

The problem is that while our self-image (as a modernist 1960s black-and-white film guy or a huge foodie) is fixed and somewhat rigid, our actual self and our aesthetic preferences are much more fluid and flexible. They change constantly, partly as a response of social pressure (see the previous answer) and partly as a result of the mere exposure effect, the well-established psychological phenomenon that mere exposure to a stimulus (say, a musical piece or a kind of food) makes you like this kind of stimulus more.

There's a fair amount of experimental support for this claim that our aesthetic preferences change constantly and radically. According to recent findings, aesthetic preferences are the most stable in middle-aged people, and they're much more fluid in younger and, somewhat surprisingly, older age groups. But even the aesthetic preferences of people in the most stable age group undergo at least one major change as often as every two weeks in an aesthetic domain they really care about.

The experimenters asked the subjects about their favorite art form, and when they chose, say, landscape painting, they were presented with seemingly random examples of landscape paintings. They had to rate these (alongside other pictures). Then, two weeks later, they had to rate the very same examples (again, alongside other pictures), and the rating was very different from what it was two weeks before. It's not that the rating was random. On any one day, the subjects were very consistent in the way they rated the artworks. But their ratings changed in the course of two weeks. This worked only for artworks that the subjects were not familiar with.

In short, our aesthetic preferences change. If you take your aesthetic self-image very seriously, then given that this self-image doesn't change (or changes very slowly), you'll end up feeling guilty when you indulge in guilty pleasures. If you take your aesthetic self-image less seriously, you'll have less reason to feel guilty when you deviate from your aesthetic comfort zone. Just as it's a good idea to be less judgmental toward others with different aesthetic taste, it's an even better idea to be less judgmental toward yourself even if you make some surprising, unexpected, and maybe questionable aesthetic choices.

1.5. Fifth Answer: We Care about Aesthetic Judgments

The first four answers were mainly dismissive: we don't *really* care. Or, if we do, we care for the wrong (that is, nonaesthetic) reasons. And the first four answers are widespread in sociology and related fields, but not so much in philosophical aesthetics.

Let's switch gears now. In philosophical aesthetics (at least in the Western tradition), the most widespread way of answering the question about why we care is in terms of aesthetic judgment. This, unlike the previous four answers, is not a dismissive one—we care about the aesthetic for deeply aesthetic reasons: in order to make aesthetic judgments.

Aesthetic judgments are statements, made to others or to oneself, about the aesthetic properties of something—about its beauty, grace, or ugliness. Ranking and comparison rely on judgments. If you think that Frida Kahlo was a better painter than Diego Rivera or that coffee is better if it's made with under-roasted beans, these comparative statements are rooted in aesthetic judgments. And posting about your ten favorite films or novels or restaurants on social media also relies on aesthetic judgments. We also often make noncomparative aesthetic judgments (sometimes just to ourselves) about the film we just watched (for example, that it was awful).

This approach has its origins in the writings of the two main historical figures of Western aesthetics: David Hume and Immanuel Kant. Kant's grand oeuvre on aesthetics is the *Critique of Judgment*, and it's an analysis of aesthetic judgment (which is, according to him, very different from other kinds of judgment). And Hume's main concern is about the similarities and differences between the aesthetic judgments of different people.

Aesthetic judgment is important—we clearly like to advertise our aesthetic judgments, for example, on social media, as we think they say something meaningful and crucial about us. But they're not *that* important. It's difficult to see why we would care about the aesthetic and spend a lot of time and money on aesthetic endeavors just in order to make aesthetic judgments.

Would we read a novel for several days or look at a painting for half an hour or watch nine seasons of a sitcom only in order to pronounce an aesthetic judgment? This seems like an extreme time investment for the purposes of making an aesthetic judgment. And if it's the making of the judgment that we care about, then why spend half an hour in front of the painting? We could make this judgment much more quickly, so we can then move on to make another aesthetic judgment. But that's blatantly not what we actually do.

To make things even worse, we often suspend judgment. We spend some time with an artwork, but we just can't make up our mind about its aesthetic merits. So we suspend judgment. This doesn't take anything away from how valuable we've found the entire aesthetic enterprise. Whether our aesthetic engagement culminates in an aesthetic judgment is irrelevant.

Making a judgment is not particularly fun, and making an aesthetic judgment isn't that much fun either. Nor is it aesthetic judgment that seems to matter to us personally. Making an aesthetic judgment and moving on doesn't exactly capture why we take aesthetic phenomena to matter to us personally.

Take love as an analogy—an old but helpful analogy, as it takes the personal urgency of the aesthetic seriously. Being in love isn't a matter of making judgments: if I'm in love, I might make judgments about my loved one like "she's neat," but this doesn't capture what it means to be in love. Same with aesthetics: we have a deep personal connection to some aesthetic objects, and this deep personal connection can't be exhausted by making judgments about it.

One could broaden the conception of aesthetic judgment and argue that aesthetic judgments are not just snap statements about aesthetic merits and demerits, for they're, say, intertwined with the experiences we have (this was, roughly, Kant's approach). While this line is more promising, it then becomes unclear what role judgments end up playing here. If an experience/judgment hybrid is what we value, we should then ask whether it's the experience or the judgment that we really care about. And I want to argue that it's the former.

1.6. Sixth Answer: We Care about Aesthetic Experiences

We care about the aesthetic domain because of the experiences we get out of engaging with it. That's why we are willing to pay a lot of money on aesthetic endeavors: experiences are worth paying for. And that's why we spend a lot of time on them as well. And it's the meaningful and personal nature of these experiences that explain why and how aesthetic objects matter to us personally.

I said that aesthetic judgments are not much fun. But aesthetic experiences are. And here I need to emphasize that what I mean by "aesthetic experience" isn't some kind of ecstasy-like hyperventilating state of rapture. Aesthetic experience can be like that, but it doesn't have to be. Many of our aesthetic experiences are rather mild: when we find the clash between the color of your socks and pants jarring or pleasing to look at, for example.

A lot has been written about aesthetic experiences, and the last thing I would want to do here is to take sides in the intricate debates about what would and what would not count as an aesthetic experience. So I want to use a very generous way of thinking about aesthetic experiences. Aesthetic experiences are often (but not always) emotionally charged. Aesthetic experiences often (but not always) have something to do with beauty. They are often (but not always) detached from our prosaic goals and desires. And they often (but not always) get us to continue trying to keep them going.

What's in common among all aesthetic experiences? My minimalist conception is that when we have an aesthetic experience, we don't just attend to the object we see. We also attend to the quality of our experience. Importantly, we attend to the relation between the two.

Attending to the relation between the object we see and the quality of our experience is special. In the vast majority of cases, we only attend to the objects we are interacting with—the kettle, the tea leaves, the cup. But it also happens—much more rarely— that we attend to how seeing something hits us. But attending to how seeing something hits us is exactly attending to the relation between this something and how experience (how seeing this thing hits us).

It's important that, according to this minimalist account of aesthetic experience, we're not just attending to our own experience—we don't just direct our eyes inward. And we're not just attending to the object we see. We're attending to both at the same time. Looking at an artwork is a good example. You're attending to the painting, but not just the painting; you also monitor how the painting makes you feel—and, crucially, what aspects of the painting have what effect on you. But more prosaic aesthetic experiences work in a very similar manner. Buying new shoes and tying your tie before a job interview are admittedly milder forms of aesthetic experiences. But both involve attending to the relation between what you see and the quality of your experience. You look in the mirror, see how you like what you see, change accordingly, look again. . . . Both experiences may and very often do involve more than this. You may wonder whether the shoes are waterproof or whether your potential employer will care about just how nicely you can tie your tie. But if you're not attending to the relation between the object (shoes, tie) and the quality of your experience, then the whole exercise is futile.

There are many ways of attending to the relation between the object you see and the quality of your experience. One historically influential form of aesthetic experience is often described as detached or disengaged experience. A lot has been written about experiences of this kind, and about what experiences of this kind are supposed to be detached from—maybe from our practical interests and maybe also our conceptual schemes.

Susan Sontag, the American writer and critic, summarized this form of aesthetic experience very succinctly as "detached, restful, contemplative, emotionally free, beyond indignation and approval." I myself argued that what's special about this form of aesthetic experience is that our attention is open-ended and distributed among the many properties of the object we are looking at. And this distributed attention is one form (but not the only form) of attending to the relation between the perceived object and the character of our own experience.

It's absolutely crucial, however, that the form of aesthetic experience that Sontag is talking about is just one form of aesthetic experience among many. It may have been influential in a specific time period (roughly, the nineteenth and twentieth centuries) in a specific part of the world (roughly, the "West"). But there are very many other experiences that would count as aesthetic in the sense that they involve attention to the relation between the perceived object and the quality of our experience of this object.

Different people who lived in different times and in different parts of the world have different kinds of aesthetic experiences. There are enormous cross-cultural variations in aesthetic experiences. And not just cross-cultural ones but also cross-generational ones. What you consider an important aesthetic experience will probably be very different from what your grandfather considers an important aesthetic experience, and not just because your musical taste is different. The reason for this variability is that aesthetic experience, like all other kinds of experience, depends on a wide variety of one's background beliefs. It also depends on what you are trying to do in order to have this experience (something that will play a central role later).

Nonetheless, in spite of all these cross-cultural and cross-generational differences, aesthetic experience in all aesthetic traditions I'm familiar with has the very basic structure of attending to the relation between the perceived object and the quality of our experience of this object. Take, for example, the central concept of Sanskrit aesthetics (influential not only in India but also in Indonesia and East Africa), *rasa*. *Rasa* is the savoring of the emotional flavor of our experience. This is clearly a metaphorical description, but what does most of the work is the concept of savoring. When you savor a meal, you attend to the contrasts and comparisons of a number of different experiences (of the ingredients but also of smells, visual experiences, and so on). In other words, you attend to the relation between the food and your experience of the food.

To put it extremely simply, when you have an aesthetic experience, you attend to how something hits you. This characterization is simple enough to capture our aesthetic experience, no matter how trivial they may be. And it's aesthetic experience in this sense that matters to us personally. In the rest of this chapter, I'll argue that aesthetic experiences (like all experiences we care about) are very often achievements. And in order to fully appreciate how much we care about aesthetic experiences, we need to understand in what way they can count as achievements.

2. Aesthetic Experience as Achievement

Experiences don't just happen to us. We very often work hard to have experiences of a certain kind. And not just in aesthetics.

Take emotional experiences, for example. While it would be tempting to say that emotions just sweep us away and we're just passive subjects of our emotions, this isn't true. We often actively try to have certain emotions. We try hard to feel appropriately sad at funerals and appropriately happy at parties. I understand that religious experience is also something that religious people often try hard to come by.

This is even more salient when it comes to aesthetic experiences. When we go to a gourmet restaurant, we spend quite a bit of energy on savoring the food we eat. At wine tasting events, we try hard to appreciate the flavors. And we spend much of our teenage years trying to really get the music we are listening to. An important aspect of understanding aesthetic experience is to understand what we do when we're trying to have it.

Not all aesthetic experiences are achievements, but many of them are. Just like not all emotions are feelings you're actively working on, but some are. And just as we can't fully understand our emotional life without taking into consideration how we often try hard to have certain emotions, we can't fully understand our aesthetic life without understanding the role achievement plays in aesthetic experiences. There are aesthetic experiences that just blow us away without us trying to do anything at all; they just knock us off our feet. No achievement needed here, but this doesn't mean that we can just ignore the achievement aspect of aesthetic experiences: we often need to try hard to keep on having an aesthetic experience in order not to lose it, and then we also need to work hard to re-create it on another day. You can never take achievement out of the equation.

It's important to clarify that, in the case of aesthetic experiences, we very rarely know exactly what kind of experience we're trying to achieve. Most of the time, we have some very vague ideas only about the experience we're trying to have. But that's it, nothing more specific. When you're trying to feel sad at a funeral, you have a fairly specific idea about the emotional state you want to be in. But not when trying to have an aesthetic experience. When having an aesthetic experience, we're trying to achieve something, but we're not quite sure what we're trying to achieve.

Taking aesthetic experience to be an achievement is important for at least three reasons. The first is that your technique for trying to have aesthetic experiences may be very different from mine. Trying to have an aesthetic experience is often a mental action. You concentrate, pay attention to some things, and ignore others. But it can also be a bodily action: closing your eyes when listening to music or maybe standing as close to a painting as possible to take it in.

And we learn from an early age how to perform these actions, and which action is to be performed under what circumstances. We presumably observe our parents, caregivers, and peers trying to have aesthetic experiences, and then we imitate them in order to achieve the same. But very often our patterns of trying to achieve aesthetic experiences derive directly from something we read or hear. And sometimes we just try anything we can think of.

Another confessional moment: I started listening to free jazz and atonal music way too early and, to be honest, fully out of snobbery. I didn't particularly enjoy doing so. But I thought that this was just a sign of my weakness and inferior musical taste that I preferred more melodic pieces. So I forced myself to listen to challenging, somewhat cacophonic music and tried everything I could to take pleasure in it, initially with very moderate success. I now genuinely enjoy listening to music of this kind, but I'm not sure I would if I hadn't tried desperately, mostly unsuccessfully, and for all the wrong reasons, to have an aesthetic experience when doing so.

This is another reason why aesthetic experiences vary wildly depending on our personal and cultural background. Just what kind of aesthetic experience you have depends on how you're trying to achieve it. And this depends on the techniques you learn throughout your life.

Some aesthetic experiences need a lot of work. Others need less. The importance of achievement in aesthetic experience does not mean that those experiences that require more achievement—like my encounter with free jazz and atonal music—are somehow better or superior or more rewarding aesthetic experiences. Aesthetic experience that just knocks you off your feet without your trying to do anything can be just as rewarding. There's no hierarchy of aesthetic experiences.

The second reason why thinking of aesthetic experience as an achievement is important is that it helps us to understand the widespread phenomenon of aesthetic experience going wrong. When we're trying to have an aesthetic experience, we often fail. You go to a concert of an artist you really like, but you just can't enjoy any of it, maybe because you're distracted or you're there with the wrong person. Or you stare at your favorite painting in the museum, which you've had many aesthetic experiences of, but today, for some reason, it's just not happening. Or you go to your favorite restaurant, but it's a business lunch and you're too busy trying to impress your boss, and you don't enjoy your favorite dish at all.

In these cases, we tend to blame ourselves. It's because of our own shortcomings that the aesthetic experience didn't happen. The painting is the same as before, as is the food you ordered. But we're not doing what we should be doing and that's why the aesthetic experience isn't happening. And on these occasions, it's even more salient how we tend to try harder to make sure that the aesthetic experience does happen in the end.

All this shows that we don't have full control over our aesthetic experiences. I've emphasized the active aspects of having an aesthetic experience: that we often try hard to have an aesthetic experience of a certain kind. But this shouldn't mislead us into thinking that it's all up to us. We can put ourselves in a situation that is more conducive of having an aesthetic experience, but we can't guarantee it.

In this sense, having an aesthetic experience is very different from, say, the experience of the color red. When you put a piece of red paper in front of my eyes, I'll have an experience of the color red (bracketing color blindness and odd illumination). But no matter what aesthetic object you put in front of my eyes, even if it's my very favorite artwork, the aesthetic experience isn't guaranteed. Aesthetic experience is a fragile state—it's difficult to achieve, and this is part of the reason why achieving it could feel like a big deal.

This brings us to the third and in some sense the most important reason why taking aesthetic experience to be an achievement is a crucial step in understanding why aesthetics matters. It matters because it is something *you* have achieved. It reveals something about yourself. There's a sense of accomplishment, that is, a sense of what *you* have accomplished. In some ways, aesthetic experience is as much about you as it is about the aesthetic object.

Remember that part of what we're trying to understand here is why aesthetics matters for us: why we take it to be such an important part of who we are. If we think of aesthetic experience as an achievement, this question is easy to answer. Aesthetic experience establishes a two-way interaction between you and the aesthetic object (where the aesthetic object could be an artwork, a landscape, a person, or a burrito). Not all experiences are two-way interactions. When you have a toothache, there's not much of a back and forth. No achievement is needed to feel your toothache. The same is true with the color red. If you put a piece of red paper in front of my eyes, no special achievement is needed for me to experience red. These are one-way experiences.

But aesthetic experiences are two-way interactions, in the sense that you are trying various ways of getting closer to the aesthetic object, sometimes failing, sometimes succeeding. You feel the pull of the aesthetic object and you try to follow it, but this doesn't always succeed.

3. Aesthetic Experience as Social Glue

We care about aesthetics because we care about having aesthetic experiences. And, most of the time, we care about having aesthetic experiences together. Sitting next to each other in the movies, dancing, listening to music together. We like to have aesthetic experiences when people we care about have similar aesthetic experiences.

Aesthetic experiences can bring us closer to each other. Listening to the same music can be a binding experience, as long as you both have the same kind of experience. And nothing can be as alienating as having radically different aesthetic experiences when listening to the same music or watching the same film.

When it comes to the importance of aesthetics for our social self, it's experiences that matter, not aesthetic agreements or disagreements. This isn't to say that we don't give a damn about whether our loved ones agree with us in our aesthetic judgments. But, as we have seen earlier, we care so much more about what kind of experiences they have when we show them our favorite film or music.

The importance of shared aesthetic experiences for us won't come as a surprise if we take seriously the idea that aesthetic experience is an achievement. If aesthetic experience is an achievement, then shared aesthetic experience is a joint achievement. And just as joint achievements can feel like a very strong bond between two people, the same is true of shared aesthetic experiences. We care about shared aesthetic experiences at least partly because, being joint achievements, they strengthen the bond between us. They're the real social glue.

Notes and Further Reading

1.1. The findings about the importance of aesthetic preferences for the self started with the publication of Nina Strohminger and Shaun Nichols, "The Essential Moral Self," *Cognition* 131, no. 1 (2014): 159–171, and various responses to this paper.

1.2. The main source of Adorno's dismissive thoughts about film can be found is his 1951 book, *Minima Moralia: Reflections from Damaged Life*, trans. E. F. N. Jephcott (Verso, 2020).

1.3. Pierre Bourdieu's most important book on the sociology of aesthetics is *Distinction: A Social Critique of the Judgement of Taste*, trans. Richard Nice (Harvard University Press, 1984).

1.4. On guilty pleasures, see Kris Goffin and Florian Cova, "An Empirical Investigation of Guilty Pleasures," *Philosophical Psychology* 32, no. 7 (2019): 1129–1155. On mere exposure effect experiments in the context of aesthetics, see James E. Cutting, "The Mere Exposure Effect and Aesthetic Preference," *New Directions in Aesthetics, Creativity, and the Arts*, ed. Paul Locher, Colin Martindale, and Leonid Dorfman (Baywood, 2007), 33–46. Also see Bence Nanay, "Perceptual Learning, the Mere Exposure Effect, and Aesthetic Antirealism," *Leonardo* 50, no. 1 (2017): 58–63 and Aaron Meskin, Mark Phelan, Margaret Moore, and Matthew Kieran, "Mere Exposure to Bad Art," *British Journal of Aesthetics* 53, no. 2 (2013): 139–164. The findings about changes in our aesthetic preferences are reported in Cameron Pugach, Helmut Leder, and Daniel J. Graham, "How Stable Are Human Aesthetic Preferences Across the Lifespan?" *Frontiers in Human Neuroscience* 11, no. 289 (2017): 1–11. For the general phenomenon of conflict between the rapidly changing self and the stable self-image, see Bence Nanay, *The Fragmented Mind* (W. W. Norton, 2022).

1.5. Hume's essay is "Of the Standard of Taste" (1757). A modernized English version is available at http://www.earlymoderntexts.com/assets/pdfs/hume1757essay2.pdf. For Kant's account of aesthetic judgment, see the *Critique of the Power of Judgement*, trans. Paul Guyer and Eric Matthews (Cambridge University Press, 2000). On how aesthetic engagement is like love, see Nick Riggle, "On the Aesthetic Ideal," *British Journal of Aesthetics* 55, no. 4 (2015): 433–447.

1.6. The Sontag quote is from her "On Style," *Against Interpretation* (Farrar Straus Giroux, 1986), 27. For more on distributed attention and the role it plays in aesthetic engagement, see Bence Nanay, *Aesthetics as Philosophy of Perception* (Oxford University Press, 2016) and Bence Nanay, *Aesthetics: A Very Short Introduction* (Oxford University Press, 2019). On Sanskrit aesthetics and *rasa* theory, see Sheldon Pollock, ed., *A Rasa Reader* (Columbia University Press, 2016). A good introduction is Kathleen Higgins, "An Alchemy of Emotion: *Rasa* and Aesthetic Breakthroughs," *Journal of Aesthetics and Art Criticism* 65, no. 1 (2007): 43–54.

2. A good philosophical treatment of achievement (which uses a slightly different concept of achievement from the one I do) is Gwen Bradford's *Achievement* (Oxford University Press, 2015). C. Thi Nguyen likens aesthetic engagement to playing games and relates it to a type of achievement in "Autonomy and Aesthetic Engagement," *Mind* 129 (2020): 1127–1156.

3. An excellent account of the social aspects of aesthetic engagement that doesn't focus exclusively on aesthetic agreements and disagreements is Dominic McIver Lopes, *Being for Beauty: Aesthetic Agency and Value* (Oxford University Press, 2018).

2

Aesthetic Lives

Individuality, Freedom, Community

Nick Riggle

1. A World Without?

A vivid way to think about how and why certain things matter is to imagine life without them.

Imagine a world in which everyone knows everything. Everyone knows all of the historical facts, mathematical facts, astronomical, physical, and biological facts. It's not too difficult to imagine. Some of the people you know know a lot of things. Now imagine that everyone knows everything.

It's even easier to imagine a world where hardly anyone knows anything. Everyone is forgetful, superficial, bad at math, clumsy at designing scientific experiments, and uninterested in the cosmos. In this dark world, humans can't share information or rely on each other for understanding. Where ignorance reigns, suffering and paranoia swarm, confidence flags, and judgment fails.

Let's try another one: imagine a world where everyone always does the right thing. Everyone is morally excellent. People might be tempted to err now and then, but temptation never prevails. Respect and mutual consideration reign. Kindness and generosity rule the day.

It's even easier to imagine a world where everyone always does the wrong thing. Just think of the worst person you know of.

Aesthetic Life and Why It Matters. Dominic McIver Lopes, Bence Nanay, and Nick Riggle, Oxford University Press. © Oxford University Press 2022. DOI: 10.1093/oso/9780197625798.003.0003

Multiply them and imagine a world full. In that terrible world, life is nothing. Pain festers, love shrivels, and friendship fades away.

Let's put these thoughts together and imagine a world that's epistemically and morally perfect: people enjoy free and open access to information; everyone is educated; they are quick to understand information, reliably generate it, and responsibly share it. And they use it to morally excellent effect. They treat each other well, look out for each other, and help each other along. Health and peace prevail. Jobs are secure and economies soar.

This sounds like an excellent place to live. You'd be healthy and educated; kind and thoughtful people would be there for you; you'd be one of them; you'd have social respect and personal love; you'd live free from oppression and free from the fear of it. What more could you want?

As good as this world sounds, it's not good enough. A flourishing world that's epistemically and morally perfect might be a world without beauty or aesthetic value.

Who cares if things are aesthetically bad? Family, safety, peace, employment—they are secure. Aren't those the things that really matter? Who cares if people aren't imaginative and creative, the art is mediocre, style bores, music fizzles, neighborhoods are bland, and sunsets are boring?

The answer is that, whether you know it or not, you care. You care because you're a human being among other human beings. To understand why aesthetic value matters, we have to understand what it is to be human.

But first we have to understand food.

2. Food

Aesthetic value is like food.

First of all, *mmmmm fooood*. Food is life; it's comfort. It's friends, fun, freedom. Food is work and pleasure—it's growth, earth, challenge, and cheer. Food is us. Without it, we die. With it, we can do anything: we can nourish, we can work, we can create, we can party, we can learn, we can love.

But what is food? I know that Cheetos, green juice, chipotles, and mayonnaise are food, and I know that rocks, bags, clouds, and universities are not food. But what makes all of the food things food and all of the other things just other things? This is a philosophical question. Not, what are examples of it? But, what is it?

I love food and I'm a philosopher, so I've thought a lot about what food is. Here's my answer: Food is whatever's worth eating. The thought is not that food is essentially something else—edible, nutritious, or delicious—and then because of that it's worth eating. No, my thought is that food just is what's worth eating, where eating is an important social practice.

Let's go deeper into this thought.

People eat. We graze, gorge, stuff, slurp, swallow, chomp, nibble, and chew. We eat in a daze, a frenzy, with or without thought, casually, slowly, grossly, politely. We eat for ceremony, ritual, and religion. We eat when we're sad, happy, suffering, and celebratory. We eat to work, for fun, or just because.

Food has nutrients that our bodies need to stay healthy—nothing could be more obvious about food in general. But it would be a mistake to think that something is food if, and only if, it is ingestible and nutritious. Some things that we think are worth eating are ingestible but hardly nutritious: popcorn, candy, commodity white bread, soda, diet soda, sugary cereal. And many nutritious and edible things are not worth eating: human flesh, pets, clay, elephant blood, and, I dare say, maggots.

We eat some things that aren't nutritious, and we don't eat some things that are, because eating is not just a matter of chomping and swallowing. Eating is not feeding. We all merely feed sometimes, and doing so is good because it keeps us alive and hopefully feels good. It can even be fun to merely feed—to wolf down a delicious burrito or go hard on a giant bowl of mac 'n' cheese. But in general there's a profound difference between eating and masticating nutritious (even delicious) matter to maintain homeostasis.

Eating is a complex social practice, and food is whatever is worthy of anchoring and promoting this complex practice. To flesh out this idea—to develop this "theory" of food—we need to answer two important questions: What is the social practice of eating? And what makes something "worthy" of being a part of such a practice?

To understand what it is to be worthy of eating in general, it helps to understand what people have treated as worthy of eating. In other words, we should look at actual ways that human beings have loved food and incorporated eating into the fabric of their lives. We can't assume that all actual eating practices are, or have been, good for those who engage in them. Some have been so poor as to hardly count as an eating practice rather than a feeding practice, and even many mere feeding practices have been awful (sometimes by malicious design). But many eating practices have flourished and played a central role in the lives of flourishing peoples.

Luckily, since you and I are human beings, it's not too difficult to study an eating practice. Look in the mirror, in your fridge, at social media, look around. Whether or not you think much about it, you are already part of, and deeply engaged in, an eating practice. That's just part of being alive and growing up around other human beings, some of whom feed us for many years before we can feed ourselves. Through their early influence they determine the shape of our eating practice in deep and often lasting ways. From a little glance in the mirror, we can see that eating involves so much more than nutrition—it involves pleasure, community, tradition, creativity, and even identity.

But we have to be careful here. While it helps to look at our own practices, it's important to understand that what makes something worthy of eating in general isn't simply what makes something worth eating for you. You can look to your own practices for clues about the nature of eating, but we must not generalize from a single case. Maybe your own eating practices are not as good as they could be! Or maybe they are good but very atypical in some ways. For this reason, we should also look beyond ourselves at other eating practices, even ones that are very different from the ones you know. Since we're wondering what's worthy of eating in general, we can look at ourselves for clues, but not for final answers.

When we peer beyond our individual eating practices, we find humans eating a witch's cauldron of things: ants, ant eggs, whole steamed little birds, roots, stems, bile, frogs, crickets, saliva, flowers, putrefied shark, jellied moose nose, grubs, rotten walrus, fermented beans, grass, cactuses, ligaments, bark, eyeballs, blood, and Doritos. If all of these things are food, then they're all worthy of eating in some sense—how could that be? Imagine going to a restaurant that only serves those things.

There's a chance that you don't like, or even couldn't imagine, eating some of the things on that list. Some people dare each other to eat the hottest, barely ingestible, peppers on earth. I haven't tasted any northeastern Thai dishes embittered by raw cow bile. I'm okay with that. Some people value eating hamburgers or ants while others value eating ramen or cauliflower. Some large and lively groups value eating whole animals that they have roasted underground for days while others never do this and prefer eating in small numbers at quiet vegan restaurants.

But we can't answer the general question without understanding how actual humans generally have valued eating certain things and the values or goods that doing so has helped humans realize in their lives. The mere fact that roots, frogs, ants, and cactuses are nutritious can't explain what has made those things worthy of eating, worthy of playing a role in human eating practices, worthy of being food. If all we cared about were maintaining a heartbeat, then bile and bugs and would be no better or worse than fish and chips.

So let's talk about ants. Abundant and rich in protein, minerals, and vitamins, ants figure in human eating practices across the globe. In Mexico, people have been eating flying ants, or "chicatanas," for centuries—long before colonists arrived in the Americas and radically changed, and in many cases erased, the foodways of the Indigenous peoples. In the Mexican state of Oaxaca, in the late spring, heavy rains hit and hordes of flying ants emerge from the ground. This is a highly anticipated event each year, and the people of Oaxaca eagerly await the first rains. The ants emerge copious and slow, easy to catch in piles, and children run around playfully sweeping them up with their families. When ground into a paste with a few other ingredients—garlic, salt, and chili are common— they make the perfect addition to the traditional Oaxacan staples, especially fresh corn tortillas and mole. Their flavor is unlike anything else, a smoky, salty earthiness with a bitter, citrusy edge.

Why are chicatanas food? Why are they a valuable part of this complex eating practice? Clearly, it's no single thing. It's due to their rarity, the fun of collecting them, and the familial, communal character of the anticipation, harvest, and feast. Their nutritiousness. Their deliciousness. The way their flavor and preparation fit into centuries-long food traditions anchored in geographically specific practices, recipes, and foodways relating to corn, seeds, rabbit, foul, and other plants and animals. The sense of identity and belonging that these complex values and practices give rise to. Without these traditions and values, chicatanas would not figure in Oaxacan eating practices. They would emerge in the spring copious and slow and uncaught. They would not be food.

We could tell similar stories about the thrill and fun of digging up and grilling tarantulas in Cambodia; the coveted Thai delicacy of Koi Khai Mot Dang, a spicy salad of raw red ant eggs; the seasonal tradition of eating wasps and wasp larvae in Kushihara, Japan. Foraging yerba santa, prickly pear, or pine nuts in the California coastal sage and chaparral region; picking apples in Pennsylvania in the fall or blueberries in New Jersey in the summer—both for pies; collecting and preparing a turkey for a holiday dinner. These ingestible things are so much more than feed or slop—they're grown, foraged, formed, and transformed. They count as food because they figure well in eating practices.

Something is worthy of an eating practice—something is food—when, and to the extent that, eating it realizes the goods that define the practice of eating. In other words, food is what sustains and promotes the practice of eating, where this is so much more than feeding because it realizes so many more goods. Some of these goods are more central than others, but from our examples it's clear that the following five are of paramount importance.

Health. The most obvious one is the health we get from eating. Eating gives us energy, nutrients, and sustains and amplifies our bodies. Importantly, though, the health sustained by an eating practice isn't purely bodily. Eating gives us pleasure, presents us beautiful things, and satisfies, affecting our moods, emotions, and mental well-being. If a large percentage of the foods in our eating practices were not nourishing of body or mind, then we would hesitate to think that we have an eating practice.

Activity. Some things that are nutritious and edible might be too difficult to grow, collect, or gather and so can't figure in an eating practice. Other things that are edible but not (very) nutritious might be really fun to gather, or gathering them might be a visual, gustatory, or olfactory treat, an adventure, or a challenging, dangerous, or otherwise worthy achievement. It might be that growing, cultivating, and collecting these things is honorable work, makes for a good job, or provides for a dignified way of life. Let's say that when gathering an edible thing is good in these ways, it's worth gathering or worth collecting.

Use. Some edible and nutritious things are worth gathering but are difficult to use. They don't fit into a culture's cuisine, are difficult to work with culinarily, don't mesh with the culture's technology, or are otherwise boring or hard to integrate because of their scent, flavor, or appearance. Other edible things integrate well into a culture's cuisine: they enhance the staples, add something missing, are fun or interesting to work with, lend themselves to creativity, or are versatile and can be used in savory and sweet ways.

Community. Edible things that are worth gathering, nutritious, and useful might nonetheless fail to create community. Sometimes this has to do with the way that ethical or religious values shape the community. For an obvious example, a group that doesn't eat meat for religious reasons won't commune around grilled oysters, even though oysters are nutritious, worth gathering, and useful. They will commune around foods and dishes that cohere with other, sometimes deeper, values—flavorful vegetable curries, complex salads and stews, embellished rice dishes, quinoa, amaranth, beans, squash, and so on. Food is a source of community in other important ways, too. In Oaxaca, chicatanas are not only nutritious, fun to gather, and useful—their seasonality and rarity make for a tradition that brings the community together.

Even extraordinary chefs at the finest restaurants in the world regard community as central to the practice of eating. René Redzepi, the co-owner of the groundbreaking Danish restaurant Noma, is among the world's most creative and accomplished chefs. Every year from 2009 to 2015, Redzepi's restaurant was in the top three world's best restaurants, and it has been ranked the number-one restaurant in the world four times. Redzepi and Noma became famous for reinventing Nordic cuisine by revitalizing what are common indigenous foodways—foraging for and cooking with the edible things that grow in your native lands. Redzepi finds inspiration in the collective and communal eating he recalls from his childhood in Yugoslavia and experiences frequently in Mexico. In an interview with Francis Lam on the Splendid Table podcast Redzepi says:

> It's such a communal way of eating. It's eating in its essence, in a way . . . This act of eating, it is supposed to be something for people. . . . People have to be the center of it. The creativity is amazing of course, but if you lose that connection with people, then it doesn't matter how creative your food is.

Chefs around the world echo Italian chef Massimo Bottura's refrain, "Cooking is an act of love."

Identity and Meaning. Human beings need food nearly every day, and on average a person eats twenty-five to thirty pounds or ten to fifteen kilograms of food every week. For the first several years of our lives, adults make decisions about what we eat, shaping our palettes and practices for years to come (and for better or worse). These early exposures to food bend our experiences, desires, expectations, needs, comforts, and memories around growing, gathering, preparing, preserving, and ingesting food in certain ways, acquainting us with particular aromas, textures, colors, and flavors. Our parents pass down their culture, their histories and practices, to us, passing down their identities to us as they pass us their foodways. Our need to eat feeds into our routines and habits and shapes who we are. It shapes our identities by shaping how we nourish, play, create, and commune around food.

Food is what sustains and promotes the practice of eating—what makes something worthy of eating is what makes the practice of eating worthy. The best foods do the best for the practice. The value of the practice of eating is complex, involving health, activity, community, creativity, and identity. A foodway or eating practice can be better or worse depending on the extent to which it realizes these central goods. And whether something is food can be a matter of degree. In every culture, some foods or dishes will realize all these values: they will be healthy, worth gathering, well integrated, communal, and meaningful. These are typically the most central foods in the culture's eating practices. If food is whatever's worth eating in this way, then we can predict that the central foods of your culture will be nutritious, worth gathering, have creative potential, and ground community and identity. We see this in the ingredients and dishes that inform the world's cuisines—from pho, tortellini, sushi, and apple pie, to tacos, curries, coq au vin, and ceviche.

Now that we have a general understanding of what food is, we can appreciate some implications.

First, it's possible to think that many, many things are worthy of eating without thinking that all of them are worth one's own eating. We all have our own eating practices or foodways; we have our own way of valuing food that plugs into our particular cultures and communities and carves out a proper subset of all the things that are worthy of eating. So you can acknowledge that something is good as food—that is, worthy of eating in general—even though you would not eat it.

Second, there's no imperative to use the very general definition of food in our own lives and eating practices. What is food in general need not be what is food for any one of us. A certain type of person—the foodie—might do that. But we shouldn't think that there's an imperative to become a foodie in our own eating practices. While the foodie might access more food-related adventures and delights than many people, such a pursuit can carry the cost of being less anchored in the habits and practices that shape a foodway and give rise to creativity, community, and identity.

Third, because food is what is worth eating, we can appreciate people by appreciating their foodways. But given the nature of food, to appreciate their food, we can't simply taste it—for food is so much more than flavor. We also have to understand it. Tasting it is part of understanding it, but so is knowing why it's loved, gathered, passed down, and important for community and identity. Appreciating food is a complex activity.

Fourth, if you really have an eating practice—if you eat, rather than feed—then your food means something to you. It means something to you because it's what makes your eating practice work, and your eating practice is a meaningful part of your identity, a source of community, creativity, activity, and health.

Fifth, food is essentially communal. This is true in a metaphysical sense (relating to its reality or nature) and in an axiological sense (concerning its value or what makes it good). Something's being food depends on communal practices—people coming together to grow, collect, create, and share food. And the goodness of food derives in large part from the goodness of community that our eating practices sustain.

Sixth, and as a result, you can't radically change your own eating practice without consequences for your identity, your community, your life as the person you are. Changing the foods that you and your community grow, gather, make, preserve, share, create, and eat is not like changing the toothpaste you use. It's like changing who you are.

3. Aesthetic Value

Ever wonder why we use the word *taste* to talk about aesthetic matters? Aesthetic value is like food! Now that we know what food is, we can make good on the comparison between food and aesthetic value.

Just as we understood food in terms of eating practices, we should understand aesthetic value in terms of aesthetic valuing practices. Food is what is worth eating, where eating is something we value doing together because it brings us an array of related goods—a valuable social practice that realizes goods of health, activity, creativity, community, and identity. Likewise, aesthetic value is what is worthy of being aesthetically valued, where, like eating, aesthetic valuing is a meaningful and complex social practice. To understand aesthetic value, then, we have to understand the practice of aesthetic valuing and say what makes something good for that practice.

Like food and eating, you're already engaged in an aesthetic valuing practice focused on things you aesthetically love. You obsess over that dress or skirt, love those sneakers, can't get that good song out of your head; you stare at the mountains near your home, feel good when that beautiful person walks into your philosophy class, or obsess over a room's lighting, design, and decor. You love certain comics or cartoons, poems or poets, writers or rappers. You love dance, street art, video games, or graphic design. You can't stand certain films or musical genres, would never wear certain things, or can't imagine liking grunge, trap, or disco.

And you don't stop at that because you also want to cultivate your love of those things. That album? You want to listen to it again, play it for your friends, use it as inspiration for your own music, stream the new one as soon as it's released. That beautiful skirt? It needs the perfect shoes and top. You want to wear it on a good day to shine for yourself and your friends. The mountains by your home? You want to see them at sunrise and sunset. You want to take yet another picture of them. You want to remember them when you're homesick or put their image on your lockscreen.

At the same time, you're not limited to the things you currently love. You also want to explore the wider world of aesthetic value. You know that there are new and exciting things out there that you might create, love, or enjoy—mind-blowing films, astonishing albums, transformative novels, entirely new ways of thinking about dress, design, or cuisine. Mysterious beauty beckons and transforms, changing the way you think about your life and self and opening you up to new worlds and ways of living. As much as you love certain bands, clothes, landscapes, and poems, you want to remain open to new beauty. You might not transform into an opera lover overnight or suddenly get into cultivating rose bushes, but your openness to aesthetic value can send you down surprising paths, coloring the way you love what you love and augmenting or even transforming your personal style.

When you cultivate your aesthetic love and your openness to the wider world of aesthetic value, something special happens. You start to excel at aesthetic connection. That is, you get better at expressing your aesthetic self, your individual style. When you do, you reveal yourself to others who create and appreciate similar things—who dance, sing, paint, dress, or write in ways that harmonize with your own individuality. But you also get better at appreciating the individual styles of others, for that is part of what you are open to when you cultivate your aesthetic openness—other people's tastes, their aesthetic interests, their interpretations of novels and films, their general way of engaging in the practice of aesthetic valuing. And you get better at connecting and communing with them even when their practices differ from your own. You can appreciate each other's perspectives, argue, try to convince each other of the merits of your way of valuing things, and cultivate a sense of mutual appreciation. When we excel at aesthetic communication and connection, expressing ourselves and appreciating each other, we generate a kind of community, an aesthetic community, that we can't get in any other way.

As we noted about food, when we consume food, we're not always eating in the proper sense. Sometimes we're merely feeding. Likewise, your engagement with aesthetic value isn't always aesthetic valuing proper. Binging a Netflix series with one eye on your social media apps, reading a novel solely to get information you need for an exam, or hanging a painting in your room to impress visitors—these ways of engaging with aesthetic value typically fall short of aesthetic valuing. They're ways of using aesthetic value for ulterior purposes, such as social recognition, distraction, or checking out instead of tuning in. Not that there's anything wrong with this. Some TV shows, novels, and movies are even brilliantly designed to be experienced in these ways. But just as it can be easy to confuse eating and feeding, so it can be easy to confuse aesthetic valuing with these other ways of engaging with aesthetic value.

These reflections on the practice of aesthetic valuing reveal the goods that the practice realizes: it allows us to develop, express, and refine our individuality, to exercise a special kind of openness or freedom, and, ultimately, to cultivate a unique kind of community. As I detail each of these aspects next, you'll notice that none of this is especially about art, traditionally conceived, and it's especially not focused on "fine art." We tend to think of art as the stuff that's in grand museums and expensive galleries. But aesthetic value, and the aesthetic lives from which it emerges, are so much more than that.

3.1. Individuality

Society has an enormous and constant influence on how you think, feel, and act. That's obvious. But as obvious as that is, society's influence can be surprisingly subtle. So many of your daily actions are strictly governed by moral norms, laws, social rules, and regulations. Laws govern driving, employment, taxes, how you treat yourself and others, and how others may or may not treat you. Moral obligations determine whether your actions are morally right, wrong, or permissible—how you should respond to your friends, act at the dinner table, or treat a stranger in need. But in addition to this, an array of social roles and norms structure how you do almost everything: how you stand in line, how you walk down the sidewalk, how you greet the grocery store clerk or order coffee, and on and on. When certain roles and norms operate in a culture, everyone tends to do things in a familiar and widely shared way. A social role is similar to an artistic genre: we know roughly what to expect from a mystery novel, pop album, or adventure film because powerful norms of genre structure how such things are made. Likewise with social roles and norms: when you stand in line, you face forward and typically abide by the rule first come, first served. When you walk down the sidewalk, you walk at a normal pace hewing to the right- or left-hand side and don't stop for five seconds every twenty-third step. A straightforward description of your actions as a grocery store customer will be largely indistinguishable from a description of mine: walked in and glanced around, approached some fruit, inspected it, and placed a few in the cart, moved at a relatively slow pace to the dairy section, selected some cheese, and so on. Maybe one of us selects different food or skips the dairy aisle, but we tend to do more or less the same kinds of things in more or less the same way. Many of these social roles and norms are good in various ways: they make society more efficient and predictable so we can carry on with more important things and not waste time arguing about who gets to check out next.

But when we abide by these norms, we tend not to be very visible as individuals—we're standard grocery store customers, everyday agents, just people walking down the sidewalk in more or less the same way. And when we can't see each other for the individuals we are, we can't appreciate and love each other in a deep and important way. Strange as it may sound, our individuality is a profound source of human community, but to understand that we need to know more about what it is to be an individual.

So what is it exactly to be an "individual"? To answer that question, it helps to contrast being an individual with being a person. Some philosophers hold that to be a person is to be a rational animal; some have argued that persons are self-aware or self-reflective beings; some have argued that persons are beings who deserve a certain kind of moral consideration. What these views have in common is the thought that what makes you the person you are is exactly what makes me the person I am: our rationality; our deserving moral consideration; our self-consciousness.

What makes you the individual you are is not the same as what makes you the person you are. Your rationality, moral status, and capacity for self-awareness are important parts of who you are, but there's so much more to you (and me) than that. Your individuality comes from how you exercise your discretionary power to value things. Some things you must value or disvalue, in general and in practice. You don't get to decide whether to disapprove of murder or whether to try to stop it (within reason). But not all valuing is compulsory like that. Some of it's discretionary—it's up to you to decide. You have your way of liking, loving, or otherwise valuing the things you value, from friends and foodways, to clothes, music, shows, athletics, and games. Your individuality includes your sense of humor, your style of dress, your taste in music and film. It affects how you spend your time, what you idealize and aspire to do, how you look and talk, even how you move your body. Your individuality is part of what makes you special, what your friends love about you, and what you love about yourself. Your individuality does not necessarily make you absolutely unique because other people might have similar aesthetic valuing practices. But it makes you interesting, special, and especially appreciable.

And it's not a fixed or isolated thing. Your individuality is dynamic—it's a complex thing in motion—and it's social. Your individuality fluctuates as you cultivate your ways of valuing. Your love for some things deepens, for others it disappears and new loves emerge. This happens in, and is responsive to, the shifting forces of time, culture, and social life. As you age, your priorities and interests change; as culture shifts its focus through political, artistic, technological, and moral change, so do you; your friends and colleagues are subject to similar influences, and they thereby influence you by showing you new things to explore, encouraging you to see anew things you dismissed, and helping you see new sides of the things you love.

As you cultivate your individuality, you cultivate a personal style that reverberates throughout your life. It shapes the way you develop and express your creative capacities. It conditions your choices and everyday decisions—what car to buy, how to dress, how to style your hair, what kinds of parties to throw, and what food to cook. Ultimately, it influences how you think about who you are and what matters to you.

In short, our aesthetic valuing practices allow us to cultivate and express our individuality. Without our aesthetic valuing practices, our individualities would be impoverished. We would live in a world full of persons but devoid of individuals. In the absence of aesthetic valuing, style would suffer, individuality would be suppressed, and we would have to plod through a more uniform and pallid world.

3.2. Freedom

The practice of aesthetic valuing and the cultivation of individuality go hand in hand with a special kind of freedom.

Have you been to an awesome concert or music festival? A beautiful dinner party? Have you danced all night with friends? Laughed your face off at a comedy show? Have you been inspired by a person with great style? Have you ever felt—in the middle of a novel, at the end of a poem, looking at the sun set over the ocean—that you were more open to the world, more in touch with the value and wonder of life, freer? What is that sense of openness and freedom?

Many philosophers think of freedom as autonomy. The word *autonomy* derives from the Greek words *auto* ("self") and *nomos* ("law"). Autonomy is self-governance. It's a matter of finding "laws" or values that you can accept and live by. We all spend a lot of time and energy gaining control over our lives. We have this control when we have good values, goals, and routines and are able to pursue them. Autonomy is what you exercise and cultivate as you figure out your priorities, work hard for good results, develop your sense of the kind of life you want to live, and live it. That's not easy to do. Real, solid autonomy is a profound achievement.

Autonomy gives us control over our lives, but it also limits us to think, feel, and experience the world in very specialized ways. Your actions, experiences, preferences, and values will differ radically depending on whether you are a doctor, lawyer, professor, have kids, live in the United States or Portugal, and so on. As good as it is to structure your life in this way, such structure can also cut you off from the wider values of the world.

While the idea of freedom as autonomy is important, it doesn't capture all there is to freedom. Our aesthetic valuing practices exemplify this truth. Our actions at a music festival, in response to a beautiful poem or novel, at a comedy show, or at a dinner or dance party are more playful, spontaneous, adventurous, exploratory, and open. In these moments, our autonomy—our normal mode of self-rule—is relaxed and takes a back seat to a more open mode of engagement with the world and its many values.

How should we characterize our freedom in these moments? It doesn't make sense to say that we're not autonomous in these moments, because we haven't lost our sense of self entirely. But it can also seem like we are freer, like our openness in these moments can augment, perfect, and even change how we determine our lives: we can reflect on who we've become, who we're becoming, and affirm, tweak, or radically alter our lives. With aesthetic freedom, we don't entirely forget who we are but we also don't take ourselves quite as seriously as we normally do. Aesthetic freedom allows us to think, feel, and act—including our creative and artistic actions—in a more welcoming way. Our aesthetic valuing practices thus jolt us out of our autonomy-governed modes of experience and action and put us in a more open state. Engaging with aesthetic value can free us from thinking, experiencing, and acting in our normal autonomous ways.

3.3. Community

When we're aesthetically free, we're more open to and engaged with the world's richness and value, to its feels, sounds, sights, movements, and scents. But, most importantly, we're also open to other people in their individuality—to their beauty, creativity, and style. When we cultivate our individuality and exercise aesthetic freedom, we can realize distinctive forms of human community. When we're aesthetically free, we can see and spark the aesthetic freedom of others.

In Book 2 of his epic autobiographical novel *My Struggle*, the Norwegian writer Karl Ove Knausgaard illustrates the connection between aesthetic freedom, individuality, and aesthetic community.

I stood in front of the CD racks. Picked out Emmylou Harris's *Anthology*, which we had played a lot in recent weeks, and put it on. It was easy to protect yourself against music when you were prepared or just had it on as background, because it was simple, undemanding, and sentimental, but when I was not prepared, like now, or was really listening, it hit home with me. My feelings soared and before I knew what was happening my eyes were moist. It was only then that I realized how little I normally felt, how numb I had become. When I was eighteen I was full of such feelings all the time, the world seemed more intense and that was why I wanted to write, it was the sole reason, I wanted to touch something that music touched. The human voice's lament and sorrow, joy and delight, I wanted to evoke everything the world had bestowed upon us.

Notice what happens in this passage: the music "hits home" when he's "really listening" and his "feelings soared." This puts him in touch with his feelings in a way that he hadn't been, and it makes the world seem "more intense" while at the same time inspiring his own creative life, his writing. He wants to have a similar effect on others.

The communal character of our aesthetic valuing practices is omnipresent. Why do we dance together when we can move in the same ways alone? Imagine being the only audience member at a standup comedy show. Why would that be so weird? The jokes needn't be different. What do laugh tracks add to a sitcom? Why are friends so important for the beauty of a dinner party when, if you were alone, the food, wine, music, and decor would be the same? Why do we want to share and discuss the excellent new music and films we discover? Why do we take pictures of beautiful landscapes and send them to our friends and family? I could go on and on. (Think about the other ways in which your aesthetic valuing practices are communal.)

The answer to all of these questions is that the practice of aesthetic valuing is a shared, social, communal practice. If you tried to have an aesthetic valuing practice that wholly excluded others, you would fail. To illustrate this in greater depth, we can look at the communal character of three central features of the practice of aesthetic valuing: how we feel in response to aesthetic value, our aesthetic actions, and how we discuss aesthetic value.

Aesthetic Feeling. We often hear that beauty is "subjective" or "in the eye of the beholder." It's not. Your responses to something's aesthetic value are not exactly subjective. When you find something to be sleek, beautiful, gorgeous, striking, or ugly, it really seems that way to you—it seems worth valuing in a certain way. You don't just like or dislike the thing; you find it to have some aesthetic value or disvalue. Of course, you might like it because it has aesthetic value, but that's not the same as thinking that it has aesthetic value just because you like it. We like a lot of things that we know are not very good: junk food, trashy television shows, vapid music. That stuff can be fun to eat, watch, or hear even while we know that it lacks aesthetic value. It's possible to like it while judging it to be bad. But this isn't how we experience our aesthetic responses. When we find something to be beautiful or to have aesthetic value, it seems worthy of interest on that account. The thing seems to shine, it seems to call out for appreciation, and our feelings in response to such things reflect that sense of their worthiness. That's to say, our aesthetic responses don't seem private or idiosyncratic. Something's shining for me or calling out to me has personal and social significance. In fact, we know from experience that people often will have a different perspective on it. Aesthetic life is like that: not everyone will share your aesthetic responses. They won't love and value the same things in the same way. And so while we hesitate to think that *everyone* should agree with our aesthetic responses and judgments, that doesn't mean that people can simply ignore our responses as "subjective," private, or irrelevant to who we are, how to understand us, and how we can commune.

Aesthetic Discourse. Our aesthetic responses, when voiced in speech, implicate others by calling on them to join us in taking an aesthetic interest in the things we aesthetically value. This is reflected in "aesthetic discourse" or in the way we talk about aesthetic value. It's a cliché to say that "there's no disputing about taste," but of course we do dispute: aesthetic disagreements, arguments, disputes, conflicts, clashes, and so on are a fixture of aesthetic life. But sometimes these disputes seem pointless, as if there's nothing to gain from going on and on about whether one rapper is better than another, whether some novel is the best thing ever written, or how exactly some film or poem should be interpreted. This contrasts starkly with many nonaesthetic disputes over factual matters about, for example, who committed the crime, whether the solar system is heliocentric, or where the keys are. Given that aesthetic difference is so common, why engage in aesthetic dispute? What is going on with aesthetic disagreement? We engage in such disputes in order to forge aesthetic community. When we engage in worthwhile aesthetic disputes, we either come to agree on something's aesthetic character—its beauty, sleekness, weirdness, intensity—or we come to value our different ways of seeing or appreciating something. Either way, a worthwhile aesthetic discussion tends to be aimed at, and when successful to generate, mutual appreciation of individuality: our aesthetic lives are revealed to each other, and we come to appreciate each other for the individuals we each are.

Aesthetic Action. The importance of aesthetic community is also reflected in how we aesthetically act. A wide range of social actions are essential to our aesthetic valuing practices: sharing, presenting, or displaying for others; inviting others to appreciate or join us in aesthetic activity; creatively responding to another person's creation; imitating the styles we respond to; laughing and dancing together; and so on. But the communal character of aesthetic valuing goes deeper than this, for our valuing of various aesthetic objects goes hand in hand with our valuing of each other as individuals. The value of dancing is more than the value of your particular movements and sensations. Part of its aesthetic value is the value of dancing with and among others—appreciating their ways of moving in the moment and responding in kind. Part of the aesthetic value of comedy is the value of laughing with and among others—seeing the smile on another's face and allowing that to amplify your smile. Part of the aesthetic value of a dinner party is the value of being with other individuals, responding freely and spontaneously to their free and spontaneous actions.

How we feel, how we value, and how we talk about feeling and valuing in our aesthetic lives—all resonate with the kind of community formed between valuing individuals. Aesthetic communities are communities of individuals who see and value one another for their individuality. As they respond to and feed off of one another, they cultivate their individuality and amplify their aesthetic communities in turn.

These are the parts of the practice of aesthetic valuing. How do the parts fit together? To really understand the practice of aesthetic valuing, we have to understand its structure—how individuality and aesthetic freedom facilitate the higher good of aesthetic community.

There's a special human bond between people who see and appreciate each other not just as the person each is but as the individuals they are. Our aesthetic valuing practices not only bring us together around shared goods—albums we both love, paintings that move us, clothes we both like. They also tune us into each other's individual style and help us appreciate one another as individuals, even when we are very different. Our aesthetic valuing practices are practices of cultivating and expressing our individuality through aesthetically free actions and reactions. Style and community are the expression and engine of aesthetic freedom. Our style embodies the ways we have exercised that freedom, and aesthetic community emerges from, animates, and rewards our doing it well. The goodness of aesthetic value derives from the value of these special forms of human life and love.

That's why aesthetic value just is what's worth aesthetically valuing. In other words, things are aesthetically good in virtue of the fact that they support the practice of aesthetic valuing: they facilitate the cultivation of individuality, aesthetic freedom, and aesthetic community. Aesthetic value just is what gives us these goods. What makes aesthetic value *good* is ultimately the good of human community grounded in individuality and aesthetic freedom.

To say that something has aesthetic value—to say that something is beautiful, sleek, delicate, strong—is to say that it's worthy of playing a certain role in aesthetic valuing practices. The "end" or highest good of aesthetic valuing is the community of free individuals. So to say that something is worthy of aesthetic valuing is to say that it can play a role in realizing this community. And so when we do aesthetically respond to something and call attention to it we do so with the hope that others will see what we see in it or show us how they see something else, maybe even something only they could see in it. As we invite each other share our valuing practices, we enrich each other either by augmenting each other's styles or by showing each other, through our own aesthetic lives, that the world is richer and even more fascinating than the one we thought we knew.

Let's summarize this way of thinking and look at some implications. Aesthetic life is a matter of having an aesthetic valuing practice in which we

(1) exercise a special kind of freedom, (2) that allows us to cultivate our individuality, (3) in such a way that we are able to create and access special forms of community.

Aesthetic value is what makes aesthetic valuing practices go well. In other words, something's being aesthetically good is a matter of it functioning well in an aesthetic valuing practice.

With this way of thinking on the table, we can bring out a cool connection between our two main subjects here, food and aesthetic life. You might have already noticed it: food can be beautiful. Which is to say: food can figure well in an aesthetic valuing practice because it can allow us to cultivate our individuality in an aesthetically free way that creates community. Exploring cooking techniques, appreciating coffee, loving fresh peaches and growing them in your backyard, learning to nixtamalize corn, making beautiful fresh tortillas, and getting together with friends to eat tacos. In so many ways, we can aesthetically engage with food.

But notice how tricky it is to do this well. To do it well, you have to treat something as both food and aesthetic value. That is, you have to value it as worth eating *and* as a source of individuality, aesthetic freedom, and community. But when we treat something as aesthetic value, we risk divorcing it from its value as food and (thereby) no longer treating it as food. If you only focus on the flavors, practices, and techniques of espresso, then you might forget about what makes coffee beans worth growing, gathering, and incorporating into lives and communities. Perhaps it's better to begin with appreciating something's status as food, taking the time to understand how something figures well in an eating practice. That will shape your individuality, augment your freedom, and tap you into special sources of community. Next thing you know, you will see how beautiful that food really is. To see the full beauty of food, it's not enough, and can even be counterproductive, to pay for the product or to geek out on one of its special qualities. You have to participate in its construction. That is one reason why we should object to certain forms of cultural appropriation, like Ikea selling "jerk chicken," or to finding chicatanas exoticized on a fine-dining menu in London.

With this general understanding of aesthetic value in hand, let's look at some implications.

First, it's possible to think that many, many things can figure well in an aesthetic valuing practice without thinking that all of them are worth one's own valuing. We all have our own sense of style, our own way of valuing aesthetic goods, that plugs into our individuality and carves out a subset of all the things that are worth valuing. You can recognize that a certain aesthetic item plugs into individuality, freedom, and community without thinking that it's something that plugs into your particular ways of living your aesthetic life. What's worthy of aesthetic valuing in general need not be what is so for each of us.

Second, a certain type of person—the connoisseur—might aspire to connect to an extremely wide range of aesthetic goods. But there's no imperative to do so in our own aesthetic lives because that's not necessary (or sufficient) for a good aesthetic life. And while the connoisseur might access more aesthetic-value-related adventures and delights than most people, such a pursuit can carry the cost of being less anchored in the habits and practices that ground style, encourage aesthetic freedom, and cultivate aesthetic community.

Third, we can appreciate individuals by appreciating their ways of aesthetic valuing. To do so, we can't simply experience what they love. We also have to understand it. Experiencing it is part of understanding it, but so is appreciating why it's loved, shared, and a source of style, freedom, and community.

Fourth, if you really have an aesthetic valuing practice—if you aesthetically value, rather than merely passively enjoy—then what you aesthetically value means something to you. It means something to you because it's an engine of your aesthetic valuing practice, and your valuing practice is a meaningful part of your individuality, a source of freedom, and the foundation of aesthetic community. We might even say we love the most central items in our aesthetic valuing practices.

Fifth, aesthetic value is essentially communal. This is true in a metaphysical sense and an axiological sense. Metaphysically, something's being aesthetically good depends on shared practices. Axiologically, the goodness of something's aesthetic value just is the goodness of aesthetic community (and of the individuality and freedom that feature in it).

Sixth, you can't radically change your aesthetic valuing practice without serious consequences for your life. Changing your aesthetic valuing practice isn't like changing your toothpaste. It has implications for how you relate to yourself, how you understand your style, and how you relate to others.

Seventh, people can create artifacts that they hope are worthy of entering aesthetic valuing practices. I like to call those who succeed artists and their products art. You can join me if you would like. But that sense of "art" is very different from the concept of "fine art" and from the concept of art and "the artist" that you might get from visiting museums and galleries. It includes sneakers and sneaker designers, interior decorators, painters, DJs, hip hop artists, improv actors, and sculptors. I invite you to consider the implications that this way of thinking about art and aesthetic value has for arts education, funding, and culture more broadly. Could it be that we need a new and more vibrant understanding of art and aesthetic value?

The way of thinking about aesthetic life developed here construes it as something *we* need and want—it is one of the highest goods we can create and tap into. But it's not something any of us is *obligated* to pursue. Life goes on without aesthetic life. You're not obligated to tell a joke at the dinner party. You get to choose whether and how to tell one. But you can simply see that *things would be even better* if you told a joke. Yet you can't tell a joke well—you can't actually make things better—unless you have style, a sense of humor, a funny joke, good delivery, receptive friends. Otherwise your joke will fall flat, sound fake, offend, or be odd or awkward. And your sense of humor is something you need to have cultivated through practice, through laughing at jokes, thinking of what would be funny, appreciating and exercising light-heartedness. When people are dancing, you can simply see that it would be even better if you jumped in, too. But if you do jump in and flail around or simply copy what other people are doing, then your actions will not amplify the tide. You have to dance with style and so cultivate something in the way you move to a beat. We can say the same about dressing up and looking good, about creating music, cooking dinner, writing literature, and watching movies together. Aesthetic life, individuality and style, freedom and community—these are all things we cultivate for ourselves and for each other. We don't have to, but when we do, we make things so much better.

That is why a world that's perfect in every way—morally, epistemically—but lacking in aesthetic value is still an imperfect world. It's not merely a world that's less pleasurable or enjoyable; it's not merely a world with fewer creative achievements. It's a world where individuals don't exist, where the freedom of openness is stifled, and where aesthetic community is scattered at best, nonexistent at worst.

Aesthetic life offers ways of living, forms of freedom, and sources of community that people haven't always sought out or encouraged. Some cultures discourage individuality in favor of conformity. Other cultures suppress aesthetic expression or condemn aesthetic freedom. Restrictive laws, strict religions, rigid social norms, racist and sexist ideologies, and authoritarian leaders have made it difficult, if not impossible, to live an aesthetic life in certain places and times. Even in fairly diverse and liberal societies, forces converge to make aesthetic life difficult or allow it to flourish only for a privileged few. This raises a big, difficult question: is the practice of aesthetic valuing something *we* need? Is it something *humanity* needs? Or is aesthetic life good for some people, some cultures, some nations, some times, and not for others? Answering this question requires a lot more work. So much depends on how we resolve issues in other areas of philosophy, especially moral and political philosophy.

But notice what's happened. Questions about aesthetic life and why it matters have morphed into questions about ethics and politics, and we have to turn to our friends in those fields for help with answers. That's philosophy—it's an activity that doesn't stop and it's one that's best done together (as we're doing in this book). Art and aesthetic value, like food and philosophy, are about something bigger than you or me. They're about *you and me*. They're about *us*. Together we create things, and we create ourselves, and through them we make a larger beauty.

Notes and Further Reading

1. The quote from René Redzepi can be found on the Splendid Table podcast at https://www.splendidtable.org/episode/670. For a discussion of food and identity, see Dan Kelly and Nicolae Morar's essay "I Eat Therefore I Am: Disgust and the Intersection of Food and Identity," in *Oxford Handbook of Food Ethics*, ed. Anne Barnhill, Mark Budolfson, and Tyler Doggett (Oxford University Press, 2018). One of the best books on food and philosophy is Caroline Korsmeyer's *Making Sense of Taste: Food and Philosophy* (Cornell University Press, 1996). Alexandra Plakias introduces her readers to philosophy by reflecting on food in her book *Thinking Through Food: A Philosophical Introduction* (Broadview, 2019).

3.1. For a discussion of personal style, see Nick Riggle, "Personal Style and Artistic Style," *Philosophical Quarterly* 65, no. 261 (2015): 711–731. Richard Moran discusses the personal lovelike side of aesthetic experience in "Kant, Proust, and the Appeal of Beauty," *Critical Inquiry* 38, no. 2 (2012): 298–329. Riggle argues that aesthetic love is a central component of aesthetic life because our meaningful aesthetic attachments partly define our aesthetic selves—see his "On the Aesthetic Ideal," *British Journal of Aesthetics* 55, no. 4 (2015): 433–447.

3.2. Different concepts of freedom have been central to many aesthetic theories, including Immanuel Kant's and his notion of "free play" in his *Critique of the Power of Judgement*, trans. Paul Guyer and Eric Matthews (Cambridge University Press, 2000). In his classic 1795 essay, *Letters on the Aesthetic Education of Man*, Friedrich Schiller makes aesthetic freedom, or as he calls it "play," central to his theory of aesthetic value. That essay is collected in *Friedrich Schiller: Essays*, ed. Walter Hinderer and Daniel O. Dahlstrom (Continuum, 1993). For a detailed discussion and interpretation of Schiller's views on freedom in aesthetic life, see Samantha Matherne and Nick Riggle, "Schiller on Freedom and Aesthetic Value: Part I," *British Journal of Aesthetics* 60, no. 4 (2020): 375–402. See also Part II, in the same journal, 61, no. 1 (2021): 17–40. For another take on the connection between aesthetic value and freedom, see Dominic McIver Lopes's interpretation of the South Asian philosopher K. C. Bhattacharya's (1875–1949) theory of aesthetic value in "Feeling for Freedom: K. C. Bhattacharyya on *Rasa*," *British Journal of Aesthetics* 59, no. 4 (2019): 465–477. Freedom is deployed in theories of irony and humor by the Mexican philosopher Jorge Portilla in his essay "Fenomenología del Relajo," in Carlos Alberto Sánchez's *The Suspension of Seriousness: On the Phenomenology of Jorge Portilla* (SUNY Press, 2012).

3.3. The quote from Karl Ove Knausgaard is in *My Struggle, Book 2: A Man in Love*, trans. Don Bartlett (Farrar, Straus, Giroux, 2014), 354. Alexander Nehamas discusses aesthetic love, style, and aesthetic community in *Only a Promise of Happiness: The Place of Beauty in a World of Art* (Princeton University Press, 2007). Andy Egan argues that the central business of aesthetic language is to come to share aesthetic views in his "Disputing about Taste," in *Disagreement*, ed. Richard Feldman and Ted A. Warfield (Oxford University Press, 2010), 247–292. Ted Cohen offers a wonderfully personal reflection on aesthetic community in his essay "High and Low Thinking About High and Low Art," *Journal of Aesthetics and Art Criticism* 57, no. 2 (1993): 137–143. Riggle's *On Being Awesome: A Unified Theory of How Not to Suck* (Penguin, 2017) discusses the "creative community builder" who uses aesthetic insight to express individuality and create community. And he argues that community is essential to aesthetic discourse in his paper "Convergence, Community, and Force in Aesthetic Discourse," forthcoming in *Ergo: An Open Access Journal of Philosophy*.

3

Getting into It

Ventures in Aesthetic Life

Dominic McIver Lopes

Just about anything holds some aesthetic interest, if you look at it long enough. Take a glance around the globe and it's obvious that almost anything captures someone's fancy. Inspired by the marvelous variety of aesthetic life, this chapter puts a spin on Socrates's question of aesthetics (see the Introduction). Why does aesthetic engagement help a life go well? Surely the answer has something to do with the marvelous diversity of aesthetic life. Imagine a future where everyone everywhere shares an aesthetic monoculture: all go in for the same food and drink, clothing styles, home decoration, music and movies, dog breeds, and jokes. Who could regard that gray, homogenous soup as adding much to life? Even if the monoculture happens to align perfectly with your own impeccable taste, I bet that you would shudder at the prospect of being surrounded by aesthetic clones. Aesthetic life matters because, sometimes, difference matters. But what is so great about aesthetic difference? Here's a thesis: aesthetic engagement contributes to our lives going well by equipping us to venture forth and explore. Call this the "venture account."

Aesthetic Life and Why It Matters. Dominic McIver Lopes, Bence Nanay, and Nick Riggle, Oxford University Press. © Oxford University Press 2022. DOI: 10.1093/oso/9780197625798.003.0004

1. Differences

In aesthetic life, we live in a way that matters by taking advantage of an opportunity to venture forth and explore. Section 2 unpacks the phenomenon of aesthetic engagement. Section 3 explains why aesthetic engagement offers an opportunity for exploration. Then Section 4 clinches the argument for the venture account. To get the ball rolling, start with a simple point. Aesthetic life is marvelously varied. That's key to the venture account. After all, what would be the point of traveling far afield, if what we find there is no different from what we left back at home? So then, why is aesthetic life as diverse as it is?

We attribute aesthetic values to items in the world—objects, events, ideas, and people. Assume that items typically have the values we attribute to them. I describe the Taj Mahal as balanced, and it is balanced. You might recall a valedictorian's speech—it was gracefully phrased. An image meme spreads rapidly through social media because it's cheeky. In these examples, being balanced, being gracefully phrased, and being cheeky are aesthetic values. They're good-making features of the building, the speech, and the meme. Of course, there are aesthetic disvalues, too: a tie can be tacky, a dance move clumsy, a story boring.

There's no mystery about the Taj Mahal's balance or the dance move's clumsiness. You can see the balance of the Taj Mahal in how it's framed by four slim minarets, and you can see the clumsiness of the dance move in how the spin ends too soon for the beat. When you're disagreeing with a friend about the valedictorian's speech, what you do is point out its nonaesthetic features. You note how she sneaked in a sly reference to the school motto, how a single phrase was repeated several times, and how she chose plain talk over fancy words with Latin origins. Every aesthetic value is "realized" by nonaesthetic features of the item.

So, one dimension of aesthetic difference is this. Everything that's aesthetically good or bad is aesthetically good or bad in its own special way. The speech is graceful, and so is the swoop of a great blue heron across the water. They share that in common. But what realizes grace in one is totally different from what realizes grace in the other. Even two graceful speeches are bound to be graceful in different ways.

This is why nobody has just one song on their playlist.

Another dimension of difference is more subtle. The Dutch artist Piet Mondrian is famous for his restful constructions of perpendicular black lines, some enclosing blocks of color, as was typical of the school called "De Stijl" (pronounced "duh style" in English and "duh stale" in Dutch). Moving to New York in 1940, he was so enthralled by the energy of the streets that he painted *Broadway Boogie Woogie*, where his usual cerebral constructions have been lit up into an electric yellow grid along which dots of vivid color seem to dance. The art historian E. H. Gombrich observed that

> In most of us, the name of Mondrian conjures up the expectation of severity, of an art of straight lines and a few primary colors in carefully balanced rectangles. Seen against this background, the boogiewoogie picture gives indeed the impression of gay abandon.

Classified as De Stijl, *Broadway Boogie Woogie* is jazzy; it swings. Classified as mid-century abstract painting—with Jackson Pollock's drips, for example—it's the opposite of jazzy. It's as cerebral and strait-laced as any other work in De Stijl. (For a live demonstration, see http://lopes.mentalpaint.net/bbw.)

Let's say that *Broadway Boogie Woogie* belongs to two different "aesthetic kinds." De Stijl is one aesthetic kind; mid-century abstraction is another. What we see is that the aesthetic value of an item depends on its aesthetic kind. *Broadway Boogie Woogie* is jazzy for De Stijl and cerebral for an abstraction.

So the second dimension of aesthetic difference is this: there are many different aesthetic kinds. Bookstores are divided into sections for classics, young adults, mystery, science fiction, and biography. The Wikipedia entry situates hip-hop by tracing its origins in other genres (or kinds) of music and by breaking hip-hop down into more specific kinds, such as G-funk and southern rap. You can usually tell a preppy from a goth at a glance because they have different styles (or kinds) of dress. Planning for a date often begins with the question, "What kind of food do you feel like? Thai? Pizza?" What we get into is aesthetic kinds.

How do aesthetic kinds differ from one another? Let's go back to De Stijl and mid-century abstraction. As we've seen, the two-dimensional design of *Broadway Boogie Woogie* is jazzy in De Stijl. Some other design is serene. A third design is unbalanced. Imagine a list of all the designs in De Stijl and the aesthetic values they realize. That's the left column in Table 3.1. What would a jazzy mid-century abstraction need to look like? It would need a very different design from *Broadway Boogie Woogie*. A design can make an abstract painting moody, but maybe there's no way to make a moody De Stijl. Suppose we fill in the table with all the possible designs and the aesthetic values they realize. Taken together, the rows in the left column make up the aesthetic profile of De Stijl and the rows in the right column make up the aesthetic profile of mid-century abstraction. Each aesthetic kind has an aesthetic profile, which is a set of ways of realizing aesthetic values.

Table 3.1 Two Aesthetic Profiles

De Stijl	Mid-Century Abstraction
Broadway Boogie Woogie—design makes an item jazzy	*Broadway Boogie Woogie*—design makes an item cerebral
D_2 makes an item serene	D_4 makes an item jazzy
D_3 makes an item unbalanced	D_5 makes an item moody
...	...

Knowing an aesthetic profile is a form of know-how. Nobody memorizes tables like the one here and then consults them in order to figure out whether a painting is jazzy or a dance move is clumsy. You're cooking for a friend, you ask them to check the taste, and they say it's a bit bland. If you're making pasta, you'll toss in some fresh basil. If you're making quesadillas, you'll sprinkle in some diced jalapeño. You have implicit knowledge of which ingredients (i.e., designs) make dishes lively in different aesthetic kinds. You know their aesthetic profiles.

Chances are you know how pug cute differs from Rottweiler cute, how country music sad differs from K-pop sad, how edgy for a prom dress differs from edgy for a costume at the Burning Man festival. These are all different aesthetic kinds, each with its own aesthetic profile, and you know the kind by knowing how to act in line with the profile.

To recap, we've nailed down two dimensions of aesthetic difference. Items differ in aesthetic value, and aesthetic kinds differ in their profiles. Both dimensions of difference matter. Nobody has just one song on their playlist, and nobody is into just one aesthetic kind.

The two dimensions of difference suggest two sorts of mistake in aesthetic life. Sometimes we miss the nonaesthetic features that realize an item's aesthetic value. Your friend misses the graceful phrasing of the commencement speech because she missed the sly reference, the repetition, and the word choice. Other times we get the aesthetic profile wrong. Someone who's never seen a pug before might have no idea that bulbous eyes and a squishy face map onto cute in pug aesthetics.

Putting the point another way, if the point of learning is to reduce error, then aesthetic life requires two kinds of learning. You must learn to see the relevant features of the item, and you must also learn the profile of its aesthetic kind.

Now for a third dimension difference.

What are aesthetic values for? What are we supposed to do with them? We tend to identify aesthetic engagement with appreciation. The balance of the Taj Mahal, the grace of the speech, and the cheekiness of the meme make them worth appreciating. This is true, but incomplete, because aesthetic engagement isn't limited to appreciation. Aesthetic engagement takes many different forms.

Think of everyone who deserves credit for the success of a high school musical. There are the actors and director, who work with a script by a playwright, while the musicians work with the composer's score. There's also a choreographer and crews for the set, props, costumes, makeup, lighting and sound, and graphic design for advertising. None can succeed in their assigned roles unless the audience and critics are able to pick up on what the production team is trying to pull off. Every aesthetic kind keeps us busy in many different ways that call upon different talents.

This year's school play is *The Addams Family*, a musical satire that pokes fond fun at "family values" by portraying a family whose values are completely topsy-turvy. In order for all to go well, everyone involved in the production had better be on the same page, aesthetically speaking. They should know the aesthetic profiles of Broadway musicals and satires. Imagine a planning meeting, where the discussion comes round to the closing number, "Move Towards the Darkness," which is usually performed as a rousing Broadway finale. Maybe something more zany and warped would be better? After all, the story ends with everyone getting what they want— Gomez sings to Morticia, "Are you unhappy, my darling?" and she sings back, "Yes, yes, completely." Could the final number be a bit more gleefully twisted than a standard finale? What would it take to realize that? Everyone involved in the production would have to think about how to contribute to the plan in a way that will bring the audience along. Moreover, when someone points out during a rehearsal that Lurch's attempt at being gleefully twisted is too cheesy, everyone needs to be able to follow the critique.

In this example, we see a general principle at work. People making different contributions to a joint aesthetic endeavor must share an understanding of the aesthetic profile. Without a shared understanding of the aesthetic profile of Broadway musicals with a satirical streak, this year's production is likely to be a mess.

To sum up, aesthetic life inhabits three dimensions of difference: different items fall into different aesthetic kinds, and people coordinate their different talents around a shared understanding of aesthetic profiles. Now that we've identified these three dimensions of difference, we can ask what it is about aesthetic values that can explain all three dimensions.

The network theory of aesthetic value is ready with an answer. According to this theory, the aesthetic values of items in an aesthetic kind are just what guide the shared and coordinated activities of aesthetic agents in a social practice centered on the kind. A social practice is a pattern of group behavior that's explained by members of the group complying with a norm or following a rule. We belong to a group that waits at intersections whenever a red light is showing. Since the explanation is that we comply with a norm, there's a social practice that tries to ensure smooth traffic flow. Likewise, in order for those engaged in Broadway musicals to interact effectively, they all have to comply with a norm that keeps them on the same page aesthetically. Their smoothly coordinated activities are explained by their all complying with the norm. What norm? The norm is to act in accordance with the aesthetic profile. Aesthetic values are the values in aesthetic profiles that explain the coordinated activities of people using the profiles.

Aesthetic life is fragmented into many social practices where people interact with each other by converging on aesthetic profiles. Aesthetic profiles differ, so the values of items differ and acts differ. Diversity is baked into aesthetic life.

2. Perspectives

According to the venture account, aesthetic engagement contributes to our lives going well by equipping us to venture forth and explore. Since there's no point in exploring except to find something different, we've established how aesthetic value breeds difference along three dimensions. The next section explains why aesthetic life invites exploration. Before turning to that, we need to dwell for a moment on aesthetic engagement. If being engaged in an aesthetic practice confines us to the practice, then the venture account is in trouble. The solution is to see engagement as one of two perspectives on the aesthetic values of items in an aesthetic practice.

Any social practice has insiders and outsiders. When it comes to aesthetic practices, insiders engage the values in the practice. They act on the values and, by acting on the values, they keep the practice going. After all, as we saw, a social practice is a pattern of group behavior that's explained by members of the group complying with a norm. Insiders keep the practice going by acting in ways that fit the norm. Even the high school musical production team plays a part, however small, in keeping the Broadway musical practice going.

Engagement needn't be a big deal. Suppose you're engaged with the aesthetic value of a bit of nature in your town. A carpet of wildflowers and some small shrubs have taken over a vacant lot and now provide a home for an ecosystem of insects, small rodents, and birds. The constant hum of activity is soothing. So you check on things from time to time, pick up litter that strays in from the street, tend its plants, and introduce it to others. Some of them engage in bigger ways, feeding the birds when it's cold and carting off the occasional dumped sofa. Even engagement as modest as this is demanding, though. Given how much good there is in the world to promote (and how much bad there is to erase), nobody can engage all aesthetic value.

Luckily, an alternative to engaging value is acknowledging it. You might introduce me to that bit of nature in your town, and I might see its serenity, but I don't engage. I don't lift a finger to help. I don't even slow down and contemplate the scene. I'm engaged with enough already, and I'm just passing through. All the same, I do get it. I get how its serenity leads you to engage with it as you do, by fending off the litter and tending the plants. I understand your perspective, though I don't share it. I'm not like someone who just sees a perfect spot for a parking lot.

It follows that there are two kinds of outsiders. Only insiders engage the values in an aesthetic practice by acting on them, but some outsiders are in a position to acknowledge the values. They can understand the insiders' perspective. Other outsiders can't see the values and so can't comprehend the insiders' perspective.

Gamelan is an orchestra of mostly metal percussion instruments that are struck with wooden mallets. When the whole orchestra plays, the sound can be so deafening that performances must be held outdoors, or in large halls, and the tempo is much faster than a player could ever achieve on their own (here's a Balinese gamelan: https://youtu.be/UEWCCSuHsuQ). My first exposure to gamelan had me flummoxed: it just sounded like a lot of very fast, very loud percussion. I knew in principle that the performers must have had reasons to do what they were doing, but they were inaudible to me. I had to learn to hear and acknowledge the values—for example, how intensely shimmering layers of sound evoke divine awe. Yet I'm not an insider. Gamelan isn't even on my playlist.

Aesthetic life pins to social reality in two ways. First, as we saw in Section 1, aesthetic values are at home in social practices. In a slogan, aesthetic values are internal to practices. Second, each social practice is populated by insiders. In another slogan, aesthetic engagement is also internal to practices. Combining the two, someone can be aesthetically engaged only in some specific arenas of aesthetic endeavor, such as gamelan or preserving urban nature.

One good way to understand a theory is to contrast it with an alternative. For several centuries, philosophers dreamt of an ideal of unrestricted, universal aesthetic engagement. On this ideal, aesthetic engagement is appreciating aesthetic value wherever it may be found, freely crossing borders between aesthetic kinds, not hemmed in by pesky social restrictions. Some would say that the elites of the wealthiest nations have realized the ideal. As former *New York Times* movie critic A. O. Scott puts it, "every culture, every class and tribe and coterie, every period in history has developed its own canons on craft and invention. Our modern, cosmopolitan sensibilities graze among the objects they have left behind." He means that we moderns can happily graze on anything we come across; he thinks we're not outsiders to anything.

By contrast, the network theory insists on the distinction between insiders and outsiders. Through their acts, insiders keep the practice going. At best, some outsiders acknowledge the insider's perspective. For them, the serene oasis of nature has nothing more than curb appeal. Put in terms of phenomenology—of how things seem or feel—the serenity of the oasis seems, to the insider, to demand that they take action. To the outsider, there's no apparent demand; it's easy to shrug off. The outsider who acknowledges the serenity gets how it can be a demand for the insider. The parking lot developer doesn't even get that.

Which is closer to the reality of our aesthetic lives, the ideal of unrestricted, universal aesthetic engagement or the network theory?

On one hand, although the ideal of unrestricted, universal aesthetic engagement is attractive, it isn't true to the fact that many aesthetic practices aren't easy to access. Accessing them takes effort and education. If you ever visit the Inca capital, Cusco, you're sure to be amazed at the exquisite perfection of the stonework, but then you'll notice that the conquistadors simply couldn't see that perfection (see Figure 3.1). They couldn't even see how laughably childish were the stones they laid atop of what remained of the walls they'd just torn down. This isn't a special case. Imagine how much trouble

Figure 3.1 Stone wall, Cusco, Peru. (Photo by Dominic McIver Lopes, CC BY 4.0)

your great-grandparents would have had with hip-hop, even if they were willing to give it a shot.

On the other hand, it's not true, either, that we're locked into aesthetic silos. We grow aesthetically, from infancy onward, and our developmental path traverses different aesthetic practices. You're no longer into many of the things you were into at the age of eight, and you might hope that your future self will look back on your present aesthetic self with more indulgence than embarrassment. Clearly, when circumstances are right, we can get into some new things, expanding our range of engagement. Indeed, every insider was once an outsider. The challenge is to square the insider–outsider divide with the fact that we aren't locked in aesthetic silos.

So how can outsiders become insiders? Recall that each aesthetic practice is made up of people interacting with each other on the basis of a shared aesthetic profile. However, the profile of an aesthetic practice can partially overlap with the profiles of other aesthetic practices. The aesthetic profile of Thai cuisine overlaps considerably with Vietnamese and Indonesian food, less with Chinese and South Asian food, and more with Mexican than with Newfoundland cooking. Many overlaps are legacies of shared history.

The gift provides paths for those engaged in a practice to become engaged in overlapping practices. Manuel has danced the Lindy Hop for years, and his friends ask him to choreograph routines for competitions. His friends win because he's good at designing clever routines that never exceed what they can do. A couple he knows dances West Coast Swing. It's a different genre, but it came out of Lindy, and he's able to create a strong routine for them, though it has a Lindy accent. Another couple dances street tango, and he won't go there: the chances of making a mash of it are too high. However, he might eventually gain a competence in tango if he ventured into salsa, which overlaps more with swing. When profiles overlap enough, circumstances are ripe for outsiders to become insiders.

Aesthetic life is path dependent. Where you are now limits where you can go next. Competence in choreographing Lindy Hop isn't even close to competence in choreographing Highland flings or kwasa kwasa. Don't hire a Newfoundlander to cater for a Cinco de Mayo feast. The explanation of how outsiders become insiders doesn't imply the unrealistic ideal of unrestricted, universal engagement.

Overlapping profiles also explain why outsiders aren't condemned to total incomprehension. The flummoxed gamelan outsider might just hear a lot of very fast, loud percussion. However, many gamelan outsiders can hear some of the merits of a gamelan performance. How much are they likely to hear? Isn't it plausible that a large factor will be the amount of overlap between gamelan and the profiles that they're familiar with? In sum, no overlap means acknowledgment is out of reach. All else being equal, the more overlap, the higher the chances of acknowledgment. A great deal of thinking about aesthetic life is marred by a pair of opposite errors. Both errors overlook how aesthetic life channels into practices populated by engaged insiders. The error of universalism is to regard all of aesthetic life as equally accessible to all. The opposite error, subjectivism, holds that there are no intersubjective standards. The network theory steers a fine line past universalism and subjectivism. It teaches that there's no single measure of aesthetic value, but we're accountable to the norms of our aesthetic communities. At the same time, we can maneuver ourselves into new communities.

3. Pluralism

Let's catch our breath. The goal is to defend the venture account: aesthetic engagement contributes to our lives going well by equipping us to venture forth and explore. Since there's no point in exploring except to find something different, we've confirmed that aesthetic value occasions difference along three dimensions. We've also seen that engagement in our home practices prepares us to go out and explore some other practices. One more idea is needed to wrap up the case for the venture account. Often, when we come into contact with others whose values differ, the result is conflict rather than benign exploration. Why think that aesthetic values invite benign exploration? Why don't they mire us in conflict? The answer is that the realm of aesthetic value is pluralist.

Pluralism is more than the fact that values differ from practice to practice. When values are plural, they differ in a way that doesn't tend to breed conflict and so doesn't require us to use tools of conflict management, such as neutrality and toleration. A great deal of our thinking about value reflects anxieties about conflict. The political culture of Europe and its diaspora was profoundly shaped by the bloodbaths that were the sixteenth- and seventeenth-century wars of religion. The death toll during the Thirty Years War (1618–1648) is estimated at eight million, including a loss of up to a quarter of the German population. True, the plagues were devastating, too, but the wars of religion were self-inflicted. Political philosophers reacted by recommending what we now take for granted as fundamental principles: the state must be neutral when it comes to citizens' values, citizens must tolerate others with different values, and rights of speech and association secure state neutrality and individual tolerance. If we tend to regard value differences as calling for neutrality and tolerance, then perhaps this is why, in aesthetic life, we're quick to say "there's no disputing matters of taste" and "to each their own."

The venture account posits that it's not in the nature of aesthetic values to breed conflict. They're plural. Plural values belong to practices that are "incommensurable," "noncompeting," and at least partly "mutually comprehensible." These are the three Cs.

Values in commensurable practices can be rank ordered. For example, the values of different types of investment are commensurable because there's a common measure of their value, namely return on risk. The investment value of a piece of real estate is either better than, the same as, or worse than that of a mutual fund. By contrast, athletic values are incommensurable across sports. Which is athletically better, a Venus Williams serve or a Sidney Crosby wrist shot? There's no correct answer to this question; tennis and hockey values are incommensurable.

Two practices compete just when values in one practice count against values in the other practice. The *bushidō*, or honor code, of the medieval samurai competes with the ideal of *satyagraha*, or nonviolence, championed by Mohandas Gandhi and Martin Luther King, Jr. Each ideal condemns the other. Tennis values and hockey values don't compete because great serves don't diminish the greatness of wrist shots. Neither condemns the other.

Practices that don't compete can still confront us with hard choices. In practice, limited resources can force you to choose which value to bring about. More tennis lessons or more time on the rink? The point is that there's a difference between a competition of values and a competition for resources needed to realize the values. It's bad enough when you only have cash for chocolate or matcha ice cream. Imagine choosing one robbed the other of all its deliciousness.

Finally, any two practices are mutually comprehensible just when competently judging in one practice is no barrier to competent judgment in the other practice. A hockey fan who can assess the value of wrist shots can also see some of the quality of tennis serves. Some think that ethical values embedded in distant ways of life can be incomprehensible to us. Perhaps the honor code of the medieval samurai was so embedded in a lost way of life that we can't genuinely appreciate how ritual suicide could be a way to restore honor (*chanbara*, or samurai movies, are a fantasy of samurai life).

Distinguishing the three Cs equips us to pinpoint the pluralism of aesthetic life. Aesthetic practices have (1) differing but (2) equally valid and (3) incommensurable but (4) noncompeting value profiles. First, as we saw, each aesthetic practice has a characteristic aesthetic profile. Each is different from others. Second, its profile is valid for the practice. *Broadway Boogie Woogie* really is jazzy for De Stijl, and it really is cerebral for mid-century abstraction. Third, the elegance of a cake and the elegance of a guitar riff can't be ranked. It's neither true that one is better than the other nor that they're exactly equal in value. To ask which is better is like asking whether Williams's serve is better than Crosby's wrist shot. Fourth, just as great serves don't speak against great wrist shots, elegant cakes and guitar riffs don't speak against each other. With unlimited resources, we're better off with both.

What about comprehensibility? That's a mixed bag. Someone into manga isn't going to be totally fazed by the aesthetics of the Tintin series. Yet the conquistadors couldn't see Cusco's stone walls as anything but barbaric and alien. Comprehensibility is limited by standpoint.

When it comes to aesthetics, we can and do speak multiple languages of value all at once. Someone can be into Hello Kitty and heavy metal, too. They're not incompatible commitments, and they don't require a split personality, with each half incomprehensible to the other.

4. Ventures

Peppered throughout this chapter are sketches of some rich aesthetic lives—of people into urban nature, gamelan, Broadway musicals, Lindy Hop. You have your own enthusiasms. But what justifies your aesthetic commitments? Part of the answer is that aesthetic engagement contributes to your life going well by equipping you to venture forth and explore. The main argument for the venture account contains two premises. First, anyone has an interest in exploring plural practices of value. Second, aesthetic engagement serves that interest. In spelling out the argument, we will need to draw upon the lessons of the previous sections.

Let's start with the first premise. You've probably noticed that your interests become rather more obvious when you find them frustrated. The philosopher Joseph Raz makes some observations that point to an interest in exploring plural practices of value. In the following passage, he is mulling what happens when we confront others whose values differ from our own. The confrontation, he writes, tends to

> threaten our commitment to and confidence in the values manifested in our own life. . . . I choose A over B, but was I right? Skills and character traits cherished by my way of life are a handicap for those pursuing one or another of its alternatives. I value long contemplation and patient examination; these are

the qualities I require to succeed in my chosen course. Their life requires impetuosity, swift responses, and decisive action. People whose life requires these excellences despise the slow contemplative types as indecisive. They almost have to. To succeed in their chosen way, they have to be committed to it and to believe that the virtues it requires should be cultivated at the expense of those which are incompatible with them. . . . Hence a variety of dismissive attitudes to the virtues of the competing ways of life.

It's a sad fact of human psychology that we're quick to regard value practices different from ours as competing with ours, even when they don't. It's another sad fact of human psychology that we're liable to disparage practices of value that we see as competing with ours. Then, if we're decent, we worry about ethnocentrism, so we try to exercise humility and tolerance. The suggestion lurking in the depths of Raz's remarks is that we have an interest in having a more easygoing attitude toward value diversity, where a discipline of humility and tolerance isn't even needed.

The second premise says that aesthetic engagement fits the bill: it serves our interest in exploring plural practices of value. How so?

Admittedly, engagement in an aesthetic practice serves many interests. Engaging—by collecting, by making, or by skillfully appreciating—sharpens the mind, provides opportunities for achievement, builds self-esteem, keeps boredom at bay, distracts from the troubles of daily life, gives texture to worship and celebration . . . the list is long. However, such interests as these don't have to be served by practices of value that are plural. They'd be served just as well by aesthetic monoculture. So, what does pluralism, and hence the outsider's perspective, bring to aesthetic life?

As we saw, aesthetic practices have (1) differing but (2) equally valid and (3) incommensurable but (4) noncompeting value profiles. Akash collects glam rock vinyl. Beatrice tends the Wikipedia entry about West African djembes. Each is engaged in a practice with its own profile. She thrives as a Wikipedia writer by getting the djembe profile right, and he thrives as a record collector by getting right the glam rock profile. Since the values in each practice are incommensurable, they can't sensibly debate whether a Davie Bowie track is better than a track by Bolokada Conde. It's apples and oranges, as the saying goes. Added to that, the merits of Bowie's Ziggy Stardust work don't count against the merits of Conde's work. There's no competition. For these reasons, Akash and Beatrice are ready to acknowledge each other's values. Neither has to feel threatened or despise the other; neither needs a self-imposed ethics of tolerance to mitigate ethnocentrism. We can easily accept—indeed, celebrate—differences between aesthetic practices.

That said, pluralism is no guarantee of mutual acknowledgment, if Raz is right. For one thing, acknowledgment requires comprehensibility, and outsiders can fail to comprehend values in a practice. More importantly, there are the two sad facts of human psychology: we look for competition between value practices, and we allow it to sour into conflict.

This is where the dual perspectives on aesthetic practices come in. As insiders, we act on the values we have, so they matter a great deal. A lot's at stake for jewelry designers, comic book editors, and fans of Indigenous hip-hop in getting their aesthetics right. As outsiders, we know how much is at stake for insiders, though the items in the practice have little more than curb appeal for us. If the practice's profile overlaps a lot with the profiles of our practice, then we might feel the pull to join in. We know that there's a path to becoming an insider. We've sometimes taken it in the past, and we hope we'll sometimes take it in the future. It's only an accident of history that we're not already insiders, and we know that our present commitments are accidents of history, too. So we also know that when we find a practice incomprehensible, there's a path to the kind of competence that will remedy the situation. Taking dual perspectives as insiders and outsiders spotlights the plurality of aesthetic life and mitigates against the two sad facts of human psychology.

Terence, the second-century Roman playwright, declared, "I am human, nothing human is alien to me." In hinting that it might be, Terence acknowledges our differences. For most areas of life, the declaration is an aspiration or admonition. Differences in moral code, religion, etiquette, and family structure either trigger perceptions of others as aliens or destabilize the insider's perspective, or both. Aesthetic lives that balance committed engagement with exploration give us a glimpse of how to get along in celebration of difference. The trick is to see that others' aesthetic values are valid and matter, even as they enjoy little more than curb appeal to us. Taking the outsider's viewpoint comes naturally with taking the insider's one.

5. Argument

The argument of this chapter has unfolded as a story, but let's make its logic explicit. After all, to know whether the venture account is true, we need to know whether the argument for it is sound, and to know whether the argument for it is sound, we need to be able to assess its premises. To do that, we should make them explicit.

The venture account is correct because, first, we have an interest in exploring plural practices of value, and, second, aesthetic engagement serves that interest. Raz makes the case for the first premise. Most of the chapter articulates and supports the second premise. The network theory is true because it predicts the three dimensions of difference that run through aesthetic life. Moreover, the network theory implies pluralism and the insider–outsider distinction. The pluralism of aesthetic value and the dual perspectives we take on aesthetic life explain why aesthetic engagement serves our interest in exploring plural practices of value.

That's a positive argument for the venture account, but positive arguments aren't always persuasive on their own. Having been given reasons to believe the venture account, you might hesitate to accept it because you have some doubts. Situations like this call for a plausibility argument. A plausibility argument acknowledges strong reasons to doubt a thesis, and then it addresses them. Removing doubt is a way to gain acceptance.

6. Sociology

You might have your doubts about the argument for the venture account, especially the second premise, that aesthetic life can serve an interest in celebrating difference. You might think that this claim just isn't true to the sociological facts. One objection is that it only fits some people, those with a kind of urban liberal or cosmopolitan attitude that isn't at home in all cultural or social contexts. Another objection is that aesthetic life is obviously full of conflict. It's an aesthetic rat race out there. Both objections paint the venture account as, well, too "kumbaya."

The first objection, that the venture account is too cosmopolitan, packs a powerful punch in relation to traditional cultures. In small societies long cut off from others, where there's a homogenous aesthetic culture, only the insider's perspective is possible. Newcomers, arriving with their glam rock and their *Broadway Boogie Woogies*, are simply going to be incomprehensible. Indeed, without prior experience of exploring plural practices of aesthetic value, insiders can't imagine how they might come to acknowledge the newcomers' values. They'll regard their own values as inevitable, not contingent, they'll see competition where none exists, and they'll be tempted to dismiss the newcomers' values. If they're decent, they'll try to exercise humility and tolerance.

In replying to this objection, the sensible move is to grant the point and limit the damage. However, we mustn't exaggerate the point. The kind of society we're imagining isn't just cut off from us; it must have no neighbors at all. Truly isolated societies are something of a fantasy. Nonetheless, some societies do get close, or they have done so in the past. Let's concede that aesthetic life won't serve the same interest for their members. Arguably, the interest doesn't need serving, because value conflict isn't a problem for them! All the same, for most of us, aesthetic life is by nature well suited to serve an interest in exploring plural practices of value. The venture account answers Socrates's question when it's asked by those for whom encounters with aesthetic difference are a fact of life. That's you and me.

This reply only compounds the second objection, namely that aesthetic life is full of trouble and strife. Perhaps folk in traditional societies enjoy harmonious aesthetic lives, but the venture account doesn't apply to them. So how can it apply to societies like ours, which are far from harmonious, even aesthetically?

The concern isn't about all competition and conflict. Actors compete for roles and tech firms propose conflicting design ideas. Competition and conflict inside a practice are perfectly consistent with explorations of value between practices. To hit home, the objection must be that there's abundant competition and conflict between aesthetic practices.

In a massive study of aesthetic culture in mid-twentieth-century France, the sociologist Pierre Bourdieu confirmed what we already sense, that our aesthetic commitments shape and are shaped by our other social identities. In Bourdieu's France, class was the major fault line: the educated and wealthy went in for abstract painting and classical music, while the middle classes went in for photography and jazz, for example. Nowadays, sociologists trace connections between aesthetic commitment and a whole basket of factors, including race, ethnicity, educational background, political affiliation, and place of residence. Perhaps, in principle, Hello Kitty is compatible with heavy metal, but powerful social forces steer heavy metal fans away from Hello Kitty and Hello Kitty fans away from heavy metal.

Recall that practices with noncompeting values can still compete for resources. Hockey and tennis values don't compete, and neither do the deliciousness of chocolate and matcha ice cream, but we might have to choose which to invest in. Likewise, Hello Kitty values don't compete with heavy metal values, but limited resources can force a choice about which to engage. The relationship between wealth and the basket of factors in the previous paragraph exacerbates the appearance of conflict in aesthetic life.

Social media also inflame the problem. They create echo chambers of like-minded people who disparage outsiders' viewpoints, where aesthetic commitment signals who belongs in which chamber. Which of the following doesn't belong? Soda pop, the Dodge Ram, Schubert lieder. Not sure? Add in NASCAR. And which of these? Lattes, the Toyota Prius, two-step. Not sure? Add in yoga. Which list is red state? Which is blue state? These are prejudicial stereotypes, and that's the point. Sadly, prejudicial stereotypes shape our attitudes toward other people. Along the way, they derail any aesthetic life that might serve an interest in celebrating difference. They make Schubert and two-step seem as incompatible as red and blue.

Since it won't do to reply by sticking our heads in the sand and denying the sociological facts, two options remain. One is to throw in the towel; the other is to gird our loins. Recall that the claim was that it's not in the nature of aesthetic life to breed conflict. To throw in the towel is to take the social facts to prove the claim false: aesthetic life is, by nature, a conflict zone. The venture account is sunk. To gird our loins is to insist that aesthetic life is not, by nature, a conflict zone: divisions in the larger society forces distort it.

Here's an analogy. Suppose that widespread sexism tends to twist and distort romantic relationships between men and women. That's probably true. We needn't conclude that romantic relationships are by nature inequality zones; we might say instead that sexism is an external force that distorts what's not inherently oppressive. Just as straight couples have their work cut out for them, we have our work cut out for us as participants in aesthetic life.

Put another way, the venture account proposes an aesthetic ideal. As long as we inhabit a world where our aesthetic commitments are made to echo other social divisions, some effort is needed to explore aesthetic practices in a way that serves our interest in celebrating plural practices of value. We should do things that remind us that different aesthetic practices are valid, incommensurable, and not in competition. For example, resisting the comparison game can help. Even better, go ahead, metal fans: Hello Kitty might be your thing, too.

Appendix
Weeds

Section 1 introduces the network theory to explain the three dimensions of difference that we find in aesthetic life. According to the theory, the values of items in an aesthetic kind are just what guide the shared and coordinated activities of aesthetic agents in a social practice centered on the kind. This Appendix sketches the theory in a bit more detail for those who're curious and don't mind getting into the weeds, but it's not essential to the argument of the chapter.

Theories answer questions. What question does the network theory answer? Manuel is choreographing a routine for his West Coast Swing friends. He finds a move that's sultry. It steams. That's an aesthetic value. The question is, why does the fact that the move is sultry give him reason to include it in the routine? In general, why does the fact that an item has an aesthetic value give an agent any reason to act?

As we saw, there are many types of aesthetic acts—editing, restoring, displaying, and writing Wikipedia entries, not just appreciating. Each of these activities has its own goal and requires its own specialized skills. Manuel's goals and skills as a swing choreographer aren't the goals and skills of a ballet choreographer, let alone a Tuvan throat singer. Yet we can say this about all those engaged in aesthetic acts: anyone who acts at all has reason to succeed in their act. Moreover, anyone who has reason to succeed thereby has reason to use their skill or competence—not to count on luck.

Manuel's friends need costumes to round out their new routine, and the costumes had better be just as provocative and alluring as the routine. If they're not, Manuel's friends will fail and so will Manuel (because a choreographer fully succeeds when his dancers succeed). Chances are slim that Manuel or his friends are any good at making costumes. In order to boost their chances of succeeding, Manuel has put most of his effort into perfecting his choreography, and his friends have put in long hours practicing their moves. They need to rely on a specialist costume maker, who has sacrificed other skills to skills in making costumes. Once we stop focusing on appreciators gazing at paintings as our ideal of aesthetic agency, we notice that people engage in myriad mutually dependent and mutually supporting aesthetic activities.

This is predictable. If someone who acts has reason to use their skill to succeed, then anyone who acts has reason to specialize their skill, boosting their chances of success, so long as they can count on others to fill in the gap. Think of how this applies all across life, to sports and academic research, for example.

In order to count on others to fill in the gap, everyone needs to be on the same page aesthetically. They all need to use the same aesthetic profile. Actually, that's asking too much, because nobody's perfect. More accurately, they all need to comply with the norm to act in accordance with the same aesthetic profile. So their specialization drives them into a specialized aesthetic kind. That's the second dimension of difference, and it delivers the remaining dimension of difference, because the aesthetic profiles of kinds correlate aesthetic values in items with nonaesthetic properties that realize the values—the slide of the hip during the whip that makes the move sultry in West Coast Swing.

Pulling this all together, here's the theory, expressed as a formula, as philosophers like to do:

an aesthetic value, V, is reason-giving = the fact that x is V lends weight to the proposition that agent, A, would succeed out of competence were A to perform act, φ, where x is an item in an aesthetic practice, K, and A's competence to φ is aligned on K's aesthetic profile.

The variables just allow us to generalize, but it helps to grasp the formula by returning to one case. For being sultry to be reason-giving comes to this: the fact that the move is sultry lends weight to the proposition that Manuel would succeed through an exercise of his skill were he to include the move in this routine, since the move is a move in West Coast Swing and Manuel is using the swing profile, where the hip slide maps onto sultry.

I promised weeds! What matters for now, though, is that we need a theory of aesthetic value as engaging socially networked agents to explain the three diversities of aesthetic life.

Notes and Further Reading

The opening sentence of the chapter riffs on Gustave Flaubert, the French novelist, who said that "everything is interesting if you look at it long enough." The nightmare of aesthetic monoculture is discussed by Alexander Nehamas in

Only a Promise of Happiness: The Place of Beauty in a World of Art (Princeton University Press, 2007), 83. A loose precursor to the venture account is Richard Wollheim, "Public Support for the Arts," *Columbia Journal of Art and the Law* 9, no. 179 (1985): 179–186.

1. The classic source on aesthetic values and the features that realize them is Frank Sibley, "Aesthetic and Nonaesthetic," *Philosophical Review* 74, no. 2 (1965): 135–159. E. H. Gombrich discusses the Mondrian in *Art and Illusion* (Princeton University Press, 1960), 367–370. The point about how the aesthetic features of an item depend on its class membership is further developed in Kendall Walton, "Categories of Art," *Philosophical Review* 79, no. 3 (1970): 334–367. Bence Nanay's work on a special form of attention in aesthetic experience can help explain how we come to see items in aesthetic profiles— see his *Aesthetics as Philosophy of Perception* (Oxford University Press, 2016). An argument for the network theory can be found in Dominic McIver Lopes, *Being for Beauty: Aesthetic Agency and Value* (Oxford University Press, 2018). On the range of aesthetic acts, see Nicholas Wolterstorff, *Art Rethought: The Social Practices of Art* (Oxford University Press, 2015).

2. Joseph Raz distinguishes engagement from acknowledgment (which he calls "respect") in *Value, Respect, and Attachment* (Cambridge University Press, 2004). On the dream of unrestricted engagement, see Larry Shiner, *The Invention of Art: A Cultural History* (University of Chicago Press, 2001). A recent argument in favor of unrestricted, universal aesthetic engagement is Samantha Matherne, "Aesthetic Learners and Underachievers," *Philosophy and Phenomenological Research*, 102, no. 1 (2021): 227–231. Nick Riggle also argues that we have dual interests in broad access to aesthetic value and in cultivating personal aesthetic attachments—see his paper "On the Aesthetic Ideal," *British Journal of Aesthetics* 55, no. 4 (2015): 433–447. The quotation from A. O. Scott comes from *Better Living Through Criticism: How to Think about Art, Pleasure, Beauty, and Truth* (Penguin, 2016), 7.

3. Pluralism isn't the same as the view that aesthetic values are determined by personal responses. For a nice recent discussion of this view, see Max Kölbel, "Aesthetic Judge-Dependence and Expertise," *Inquiry* 59, no. 6 (2016): 589–617. Classic discussions are Alan H. Goldman, *Aesthetic Value* (Westview, 1995) and Jerrold Levinson, "Aesthetic Properties, Evaluative Force, and Differences of Sensibility," in *Aesthetic Concepts: Essays after Sibley*, ed. Emily Brady and Jerrold Levinson (Oxford University Press, 2001), 61–80. On disagreement in aesthetic life, see Peter Kivy, *De Gustibus: Arguing about Taste and Why We Do It* (Oxford University Press, 2015).

4. The passage from Raz appears in his "Multiculturalism: A Liberal Perspective," *Ethics in the Public Domain: Essays in the Morality of Law and Politics* (Oxford University Press, 1994), 180. The quote from Terence is from his play, *Heauton Timorumenos* (*The Self-Tormentor*). A good paper to read about how to interact as an aesthetic outsider is Michael Rings, "Aesthetic

Cosmopolitanism and the Challenge of the Exotic," *British Journal of Aesthetics* 59, no. 2 (2019): 161–178. A book that touches on related themes is Anthony Appiah, *Cosmopolitanism: Ethics in a World of Strangers* (Norton, 2006).

6. Pierre Bourdieu's study was published as *Distinction: A Social Critique of the Judgement of Taste*, trans. Richard Nice (Harvard University Press, 1984). This is a long and difficult book. A more manageable case study of one art is Bourdieu's *Photography: A Middle-Brow Art*, trans. Shaun Whiteside (Stanford University Press, 1990). For more contemporary work in the sociology of art, try Bethany Bryson, "'Anything but Heavy Metal': Symbolic Exclusion and Musical Dislikes," *American Sociological Review* 61, no. 5 (1996): 884–899. Carl Wilson, a music critic, tells an honest and heartwarming story of trying to resist the social forces by overcoming his disdain for Céline Dion in *Let's Talk about Love: A Journey to the End of Taste* (Continuum, 2007).

Appendix. A full defense of the network theory is in Dominic McIver Lopes, *Being for Beauty: Aesthetic Agency and Value* (Oxford University Press, 2018). For a summary, see Dominic McIver Lopes, "Précis of *Being for Beauty: Aesthetic Agency and Value*," *Philosophy and Phenomenological Research*, 102, no. 1 (2021): 232–242.

Breakout

There's a lot the three of you share in common. You're all dead set against elitism, you all see the arts as part of a bigger aesthetic sphere, and you all pooh-pooh the idea that aesthetic life is about pronouncing judgments, for example. That's all very genial, but we make progress in philosophy by trying out different ideas. Let's see what you disagree about.

1. Disagreement

Maybe the place to start is with aesthetic disagreement. We disagree with our friends about movies and music, food and clothing. That can be interesting, because we learn a lot about each other from our differences. But disagreements can strain or even spoil our relationships, too. Do you think disagreement is a feature of aesthetic life, or is it a bug?

DML: There's an old saying, that there's no disputing matters of taste, but that's plainly false. Over pizza and beer, after a movie, people often argue with each other about what worked in the movie and what didn't, how it compares to other movies, and whether the rating on Rotten Tomatoes is fair. Disputes like these are fun, and they seem to have a point. The question is really, what's the point of aesthetic disagreement? Where does it get us?

Here's one idea. If we want to belong to communities of people who share the same taste, then aesthetic disagreements

Aesthetic Life and Why It Matters. Dominic McIver Lopes, Bence Nanay, and Nick Riggle, Oxford University Press. © Oxford University Press 2022. DOI: 10.1093/oso/9780197625798.003.0005

could be ways of finding out who shares our taste. Nick, does this idea fit with your thinking about aesthetic community?

NR: Many people endorse the view that aesthetic conversation is about sharing sensibilities. A similar view is famously developed by the eighteenth-century German philosopher Immanuel Kant. So, I might be an outlier here, but I disagree with the thought that sharing sensibilities is the main point of aesthetic conversation and dispute. I think that aesthetic conversations are fundamentally about coming to appreciate each other's individuality. Clearly that can happen when our sensibilities converge, so I agree with that much. But I think we can have successful or worthwhile disputes even when we don't come to agree with each other. Through our dispute, I might come think your interpretation of a film, your seeing beauty in a style of design or decor, or your love for some band is interesting, intriguing, wonderful, even if I don't share your view. A friend of mine always has fascinating takes on film. I don't always agree with him, but I always want to know what he thinks and why—I want to know and appreciate how he sees things. Art and film critics often vehemently disagree! And they also often have deep respect for one another.

Dom, your view kind of splits the difference, doesn't it, because convergence is important for you within a practice but not without? I'm also curious about Bence's thinking here. I'd guess that for him aesthetic disagreements are about which aesthetic experiences are really worth pursuing. But I wonder if he'd accept the notion that some experiences are much better than others.

DML: Yes, I do think all the folk putting on the *Addams Family* production have to converge on the goods of the aesthetic practice. The point of disagreement is to help them converge. Consider this disagreement:

G: Zara's tall!
B: No, she's not.

If G is the gymnastics coach and B is the basketball coach, then their disagreement is silly unless they're trying to figure out what the context is. Is Zara trying out for gymnastics or the basketball team? Now try this:

P: That dress is pretty edgy!

B: No, it's not edgy enough.

Suppose P makes prom dresses, but B wants a costume for the Burning Man festival. B is trying to get P to see what counts as edgy on the Burning Man scene. Their disagreement helps them to converge on the Burning Man aesthetic. I should add that it can also help them to converge on what the aesthetic of a practice is going to be. After all, disagreement is a tool for change.

BN: I like the edgy dress example, but I'd push it one step further. Yes, there's a difference between whether the dress is edgy for a prom or for Burning Man. So context matters. But so does the cultural background of the people who disagree—P and B in Dom's example. Imagine that P comes from a small rural community in Nevada (not far away from Black Rock Desert, where the festival takes place). And imagine that B comes from the Bay Area. They're looking at the very same dress, and they both know this is for the Burning Man. So we fix the context, but we could still get very different assessments of whether a dress is edgy, even if it's crystal clear that the context is "edgy for the Burning Man."

In some sense P and B still don't really disagree here: judging from the cultural background of a rural community in Nevada, the dress may be extremely edgy for Burning Man, but from the cultural background of the Bay Area, it may not be edgy enough (or maybe the other way round). It's not the case that if one of them is right, then the other one must be wrong. So they don't really disagree. We do get genuine aesthetic disagreements, but only between people whose cultural background is very similar. But that happens relatively rarely. There can be huge differences in cultural background even between two people who live on the same street (if, say, one of them only listens to gangsta rap and the other only to heavy metal). Just imagine the enormous differences in cultural background between people from different continents.

2. Subjectivism

Another old saying is that beauty's in the eye of the beholder. Is beauty "subjective"—is it just a matter of personal opinion whether something has aesthetic value? Why do so many people seem to accept this thought?

NR: I think the idea that beauty is in the eye of the beholder is attractive to many people because people differ so much in how they live their aesthetic lives. One person loves desert landscapes, another loves snowy mountains; one person loves horror films, another cannot stand them; and so on. Aesthetic difference is an essential feature of aesthetic life, not only from person to person, but also for a single person as they move through life. We're all a little, shall we say, uncertain (embarrassed?) about our sense of style or taste in music in years past.

Aesthetic difference is widespread and common, but that doesn't support the idea that aesthetic value is simply a matter of opinion. We can support our aesthetic beliefs, we can point out to others what's good in the things we aesthetically love, and we can admit that we are or have been wrong. As I argued in my piece, aesthetic value is what's worth aesthetically valuing, but it doesn't follow that everyone necessarily lives their aesthetic life well. As with life in general, we're bound to err. We can't all get perfect advice from Queer Eye's Fab Five. We waste our time on bad art, ugly clothes, sucky bands. We can think that something contributes to our individuality and aesthetic freedom when it doesn't. We can get sucked into aesthetic communities that really have little to offer. It matters that we live our aesthetic lives well. For me that comes down to whether you have good style, whether you're tapped into good aesthetic communities, and whether you're able to be aesthetically free.

DML: What's subjective is what's entirely up to individuals. For example, what's pleasing is totally up to you. If you just don't like the taste of coffee, then that's that. You can't be wrong about it. Pleasure's subjective.

So isn't part of the problem that we mistakenly equate pleasure and aesthetic value? As Nick says, we can be wrong about whether a speech is graceful or about what counts as edgy for a prom dress. The kid who sings Lurch's lines can miscalculate: he thinks his delivery is gleefully twisted, but really it's cheesy.

It's no surprise that we mistakenly confuse pleasure and aesthetic value, because aesthetic life is often a source of pleasure. Since pleasure and aesthetic value tend to accompany one another, we often use liking to stand in for goodness. I say, "I really like that," when I mean that it was well done, fresh and original, surprising at every turn.

Confession time. I know Wagner's operas are masterpieces, but I don't like them. Sometimes I'll go see a show and think, "That was well done, but I just don't like that sort of thing." I've ordered some beautifully constructed cocktails and wished I'd chosen a beer.

BN: I'm not as set against subjectivism—at least in one sense of subjectivism—as Dom and Nick. So I would say that the reason why many people think that beauty is in the eye of the beholder is because, in some very specific sense, beauty is indeed in the eye of the beholder.

There's aesthetic judgment and there's aesthetic experience. I say a fair amount about this distinction in my piece, where

I argue that while aesthetic judgments have played a huge role in aesthetics, they're not why we care about aesthetic activities. We care about aesthetic activities because they give us aesthetic experiences—not because they allow us to make aesthetic judgments.

Aesthetic judgments are statements we make—to others or to ourselves—about aesthetic matters: about whether the dress is edgy, about whether the movie's happy ending is cheesy. For all the reasons that Dom and Nick gave here, it might be plausible to say that aesthetic judgments are not subjective.

But aesthetic experiences are subjective in a very important sense of the term. Not in the sense that having an experience guarantees that this experience is correct. It doesn't. Many of our experiences are illusory: they can misrepresent. And aesthetic experiences can also misrepresent. But aesthetic experiences are subjective in the sense that I can't come along and say that you shouldn't have had that aesthetic experience. If you feel it, you feel it and nobody can take it away from you. And this is explained, at least partially, by the importance of achievement in aesthetic experiences. You yourself need to do stuff to have an aesthetic experience: you need to achieve it. So it's at least partly your doing. Even if it's something silly that you have achieved, it was you who did it. Same with aesthetic experiences. In this very specific, but important, sense aesthetic experiences are subjective and beauty is in the eye of the beholder.

3. Ethnocentrism

All three of you have grown up and work in what could be referred to as the "West." How much of your account of aesthetic life has a Western bias? Is your account generalizable to people from all cultural backgrounds?

DML: Can we use a more accurate term than "West"? Some scholars have coined "Euro" to refer to European cultures and their offshoots around the globe. How about that?

BN: I take cultural variations in aesthetic experience very seriously. In fact, one important reason why aesthetic experience varies across cultures is that our practices of trying to achieve an aesthetic experience can be very different depending on our cultural background. I think in Euro culture, especially in the past two centuries, a very specific kind of aesthetic experience was all the rage, a certain detached contemplative kind of experience. But there's no reason to think that in earlier centuries or in other cultures, this would be the kind of aesthetic experience people go in for. And it's pretty likely that aesthetic experience of this kind is on its way out. So whatever I say about aesthetic experience should be applicable to aesthetic experience in any cultural background.

But I do think that Eurocentrism might be a problem for Nick. Nick, you emphasize the importance of individuality and freedom, and while you have something very specific in mind, one might worry that at least on the face of it, individuality and freedom are almost a caricature of specifically Euro values. Is what you say applicable to different parts of the world and also to different time periods?

NR: Right, the feature of my view that's more unusual from a global and historical perspective is my emphasis on the importance of being an individual (in a specific sense). Not every culture emphasizes this. This part of my view is inspired by reflection on my own life and what I find meaningful and important, but it's also inspired by the nineteenth-century German philosopher, poet, and playwright, Friedrich Schiller's (1759–1805) *Letters on the Aesthetic Education of Man*. Schiller argues that human nature has two sides: one is the source of our variety and individuality, and the other is the source of our uniformity, or how we understand and act in the world in similar ways. Schiller envisions an ideal political state that respects both aspects of human nature. Such a state doesn't suppress citizens' individuality in favor of uniformity, but it also doesn't just let everyone run wild. Only then will we be truly free, Schiller thinks, and to get there we need to cultivate our aesthetic freedom. By cultivating our aesthetic freedom, we ourselves will be neither overly individualistic and unreliable, nor overly rational and uniform. As he puts it, we won't be "at odds" with ourselves.

Schiller was writing in the mid-1790s during and in response to the French Revolution, a time when democracies were on the rise, and he wasn't alone in seeing promise in a more "aesthetic" way of life. We see similar ideas crop up as democracies start to take hold across Europe—for example, in the French poet and critic Charles Baudelaire's *The Painter of Modern Life* (1863), in Karl Marx's writing, and others. So my emphasis on being an individual, and the conception of aesthetic life that it features in, is part of a bigger picture of collective human life.

My view doesn't privilege the aesthetic activities or products of any particular culture. I think that an essential part of aesthetic life is cultivating an openness to unfamiliar sources of aesthetic value. For me this derives from the importance of aesthetic freedom, which requires us not to be too caught up in our ways of doing things. I think Dom agrees with this in his own way—is that right, Dom?

DML: Let me say that although it's true that I grew up and work in Canada, my background is actually a blend of Gaelic-speaking Scots from the Outer Hebrides and Portuguese-influenced South Asians from the Konkan Coast of India. Maybe the venture account comes naturally to me!

If we really do have an interest in having nonthreatening encounters with different ways of life, then it's wonderful that we can embrace aesthetic differences. So why would anyone think that this interest in difference is a narrowly Euro interest? Are opportunities to embrace aesthetic difference truly unique to

Euro culture? I doubt it. Contact with others is pretty much universal among human societies.

In his wonderful book, *Vermeer's Hat*, the historian Timothy Brook describes the rise of a global perspective on culture in the seventeenth century. For the first time, we saw our own cultures as single points in a kaleidoscope of world cultures—different from all of them. Since then, walking from one neighborhood to the next in cities like London, Melbourne, New York, and Toronto is like striding across the planet.

But ventures in aesthetic life don't require that kind of contact with all. It's enough to rub up against some difference. Every group has its neighbors. Newspapers somehow forget this when they report the "discovery" of some "uncontacted" people in the Amazon rainforest. We have a fantasy of premodern cultures as pure, self-contained, never mixing with others. The truth is that they just didn't mix with us! It's our weird hang-up that we want them to be pure and self-contained. Part of what the venture account offers is a picture of aesthetic life that helps us get over the hang-up.

4. Fashion

Aesthetic life is constantly changing. It's driven by fashions. Isn't this one of the criticisms made by those who favor great works of art? Great works of art appeal across time, whereas much of the rest of aesthetic life is driven by fads. How does change come into the story for each of you?

DML: That's two questions. One's about whether what's fad-driven matters less than the tried and true. The other's about why there's change at all.

Here's a standard critique of fads. The American economist and philosopher Thorsten Veblen (1857–1929) thought that increased wealth in the twentieth century led to what he called "conspicuous consumption." That's the phenomenon of buying things just to signal prestige to others. Conspicuous consumption tends to produce fads. When everyone now has this year's style of jeans, the way to signal prestige is to wear the next style. Jeans companies exploit this to sell more jeans by changing the jeans style every year. So the critique is that aesthetic fads manipulate our behaviors, making us turn over our money, whereas great works of art are always there, quietly waiting for us to be ready for them.

One problem with this argument is that people also signal prestige by choosing to go for great art. The TV series *Frasier* poked fun at this for eleven seasons! Another problem is deeper. Why assume that what lasts only for a short while is, just for that reason, not as good? Maybe we have a prejudice for what lasts. The Queen of the Night cactus (*Selenicereus grandiflorus*) blooms for one night, once a year. How poignant is that!

By the way, connecting back to the previous question about ethnocentrism, it seems to be a Euro thing to seek the timeless. Japanese aesthetics puts a greater emphasis on the fleeting and impermanent, for example.

The Veblen-based argument also explains change in aesthetic life as driven by conspicuous consumption. I agree that's part of the story, but it's not the whole story. Here's what the network theory adds: members of a practice change the practice when that helps them to coordinate with each other better.

NR: I agree that the Veblen line about change in aesthetic life is interesting but incomplete at best. From my perspective, pressures toward change come from each element of the practice of aesthetic valuing. Consider individuality: this is something we're constantly exploring and cultivating. You have a sense of humor, but you don't want to simply laugh at the same jokes all the time.

Even if you have a settled style of design and decor, you switch it up, you rearrange things, you experiment with going deeper into the style. The capacity for aesthetic freedom adds an element of unpredictability to our aesthetic lives, opening us up to new sources of aesthetic value that can change and improve our valuing practices. And aesthetic communities are dynamic, responsive, and interactive.

Maybe aesthetic change comes from a deeper source. Some philosophers think change is essential to the pursuit of value because values themselves are things we are always in the process of pursuing. In his essay, "Fenomenología del Relajo," Mexican philosopher Jorge Portilla (1919–1963) writes that

valuing and being do not seem to ever be able to unite in a definitive manner, or, at least, there doesn't seem to be any experience or object in the area of our human experience in which this coincidence occurs fully.... Values in themselves always are beyond their possible manifestations.

I am definitely attracted to a view like that.

But in addition to this, I'm simply an aesthetic optimist. I believe in aesthetic progress. Aesthetic things change not just due to arbitrary or irrelevant forces but because they're getting better. Styles change and improve. Someone like David Bowie couldn't have existed in 1920. Beyoncé, Yayoi Kusama, Megan Thee Stallion, Guerrilla Girls—these individuals light up the aesthetic world and they light up our aesthetic lives.

BN: Instead of a contrast between art and fashion, I see an analogy and an analogy that is extremely illuminating. I don't think art is everlasting and fashion is fleeting. Changes in art— including "high art" are as fashion-driven as the popularity of Facebook memes or flip-flops. Ernst Gombrich, one of the most important art historians of the twentieth century, wrote a very influential essay on how we can understand stylistic changes in fine art in terms of changes in fashion. Painters or composers are as aware of what's "in" when it comes to their stylistic choices as you or I when going shoe shopping. Fashion has no rhyme or reason, and artistic changes don't either.

And fashion influences not just how we create artworks but also how we look at them. The way we approach an artwork, the kind of effort we put in to achieve an aesthetic experience, is also fashion driven. Here's an example. Many film critics make a point of watching films from the first row in the middle. They have all kinds of justifications for why this is the best way to watch films. I myself tend to disagree and always sit in the last row, but I've seen many young film critics unquestioningly making a beeline for the first row, following the fashion. So our practices of engaging with art are also to a large extent dictated by fashion.

I think the importance of fashion is actually a challenge to Dom's approach. Dom, your account is about leaving our comfort zones and venturing to discover new art forms, new styles, new aesthetic practices. But if we take fashion seriously, then we don't explore new art forms and new styles out of sheer adventurousness, but because someone we know (a friend or romantic partner) or someone we know of (a celebrity) recommends it. I've definitely discovered more artistic genres and styles because friends or romantic partners liked them than just from an inner venturing urge. This makes me wonder how prevalent is venturing that isn't in some sense fashion driven and whether what the venturing account explains couldn't be explained in terms of fashion alone.

DML: I don't see any incompatibility. For one thing, it's dreary and sad traveling alone! We can have multiple reasons to venture into new territory, such as keeping in company with our friends. For another thing, we can do the right thing for the wrong motives. Sometimes the winds of fashion blow us where we already have good reason to go.

5. Beauty Myths

The human body is a site of much aesthetic agony and agonizing, with people trying to meet and being oppressed by rigid standards of "beauty." What do your views say about human beauty?

NR: Given the importance of aesthetic life and our practices of aesthetic valuing, it's no surprise that people will try to manipulate us and force us to live our aesthetic lives in ways that benefit them. When there's something big to gain from influencing the ways that people think about what matters, we can be sure that political and economic actors will try to gain it. Nefarious forces tell us how to value or disvalue the look of our bodies, our faces, our hair, and in doing so they cause us to feel undue shame or pride, encourage us to buy their products, and to police and shame others who do not fit the arbitrary mold. The result is often a whole lot of bland "individuals" who have at best a tenuous grip on their aesthetic freedom.

DML: This is such a pressing social problem. I think we should consider how it works and see if we can offer solutions. The English philosopher Heather Widdows thinks two things have happened. First, a single standard of beauty has spread globally—it valorizes youthful, slim, muscled, fair-skinned bodies. Second, the beauty ideal has been moralized. That is, we've come to regard having a body like this as a moral obligation. Those who fail to meet the moral obligation—and that's almost all of us—feel shame and become targets of others' loathing. (That's how it goes with moral failures.)

I think all three of us have things to say to help us out of the beauty trap that Widdows has in mind. At this point, our readers are probably getting tired of hearing about ventures in aesthetic life, so I'll just point out that a commitment to the pluralism and diversity of aesthetic practices, which brings with it a serious openness to difference, can be a powerful antidote to the single, global ideal of personal beauty and to the obligation we feel to bow before it.

Nick, surely this is where your ideas about freedom come in.

Bence, I'm not exactly sure about achievement.

NR: Exactly. But I have to be careful here. I'm skeptical of any global aesthetic standard—for bodies, for hair, for painting, for architecture. I don't think that any individual can make legitimate demands on another to aesthetically value in one way or another. So a demand that appeals to some purported universal standard is especially bogus. But, as I said earlier, we can make aesthetic mistakes and people (often friends) can point these out to us. "Nope. No way. You can't wear that," a friend might say. Or someone might urge us to see some new film or read a new novel. "You have to see it." I understand claims like this not as demands but as invitations to exercise our aesthetic sensibilities. Invitations in general can be appropriate or inappropriate, and often an aesthetic invitation from a friend is legit. Our friends look out for us aesthetically. In any case, these are important issues that I'm still thinking through, and I think people like us have a lot of work to do.

Bence, I'm curious what you would say about personal style and standards of beauty.

BN: I'm actually a bit more optimistic about our chances to stand up to how the nasty capitalist mass media brainwashes us to have a very specific standard of beauty. Don't get me wrong. I agree that this is happening and I also agree that much of it's done for profit. But there are some psychological reasons why this is only part of the story.

We know from many empirical studies that being exposed to any kind of stimulus (a song, an image, a smell) makes it more likely that you like that stimulus more. This is called the mere exposure effect: mere exposure to a Billie Eilish song will make you like it more, even if you think of yourself as a fan of heavy metal or gangsta rap. But the mere exposure effect also works when it comes to the human body. This starts with your own body, which you see a lot, including your face in the mirror or, more recently, in Zoom calls.

But mere exposure cuts both ways. It's a means by which beauty myths are created, because the prevalence of a very specific body type in the media and in social media increases one's preferences for that body type, and this often leads to dissatisfaction with one's own body. But knowing the mechanism of how this works can also help us. To a certain extent we can choose what media content we're exposed to—whose Instagram feed we look at, for example. And being exposed to #bodypositive content harnesses the exposure effect, leading to an appreciation of many different body types and to a genuine appreciation of your own body.

Notes and Further Reading

1. On aesthetic disagreement, see Peter Kivy, *De Gustibus: Arguing about Taste and Why We Do It* (Oxford University Press, 2015). Immanuel Kant discussed shared aesthetics is his 1790 *Critique of the Power of Judgement*, trans. Paul Guyer and Eric Matthews (Cambridge University Press, 2000). For more recent work on aesthetic disagreement and shared taste, see Andy Egan, "Disputing about Taste," *Disagreement*, ed. Richard Feldman and Ted A. Warfield (Oxford University Press, 2010), 247–292. On how disagreement is a way to figure out the context, see Timothy Sundell, "Disagreements about Taste," *Philosophical Studies* 155, no. 2 (2011): 267–288.

2. The classic discussion is David Hume's 1757 essay "Of the Standard of Taste." A modernized English version is available at http://www.earlymode rntexts.com/assets/pdfs/hume1757essay2.pdf. Robert Hopkins explores the middle ground between subjectivism and realism in "Kant, Quasi-Realism, and the Autonomy of Aesthetic Judgment," *European Journal of Philosophy* 9, no. 6 (2001): 166–189. Louise Hanson argues that aesthetic realism is on more equal footing with moral realism than one might have thought—see her "Moral Realism, Aesthetic Realism, and the Asymmetry Claim," *Ethics* 129, no. 1 (2018): 39–69.

3. Friedrich Schiller's *Letters on the Aesthetic Education of Man* had an enormous influence on German culture—see *Friedrich Schiller: Essays*, ed. Walter Hinderer and Daniel O. Dahlstrom (Continuum, 1993). Charles Baudelaire's *The Painter of Modern Life*, trans. Jonathan Mayne (Phaidon,

1964) can be easily found online. In his writings on estranged labor, Karl Marx emphasizes that human beings are productive agents for whom it's important to shape their environment aesthetically—see *The Economic and Philosophical Manuscripts of 1844* (Prometheus Books, 1987). A recent discussion of autonomy and community in aesthetics is Eileen John, "Beauty, Interest, and Autonomy," *Journal of Aesthetics and Art Criticism* 70, no. 2 (2012): 172–192. Timothy Brook's bestseller is *Vermeer's Hat: The Seventeenth Century and the Dawn of the Global World* (Penguin, 2008). Lopes recommends Brian Eno's inspiring short note, "Let's Carnival," *Prospect Magazine* (March 10, 2010), available at https://www.prospectm agazine.co.uk/arts-and-books/lets-carnival. On the emphasis on contemplation in Euro culture and what it's too narrow, see Nicholas Wolterstorff, *Art Rethought: The Social Practices of Art* (Oxford University Press, 2015). Nanay outlines a non-Eurocentric aesthetics in his *Global Aesthetics* (Oxford University Press, 2021). A short reflection on aesthetic ethnocentrism is Kathleen Higgins, "Global Aesthetics—What Can We Do?" *Journal of Aesthetics and Art Criticism* 75 (2017): 239–249.

4. Thorsten Veblen's ideas about conspicuous consumption are in his very readable *Theory of the Leisure Class: An Economic Study in the Evolution of Institutions* (Macmillan, 1899), downloadable at http://www.gutenberg.org/ebooks/833. Gombrich's paper is Ernst Gombrich, "The Logic of Vanity Fair, Alternatives to Historicism in the Study of Fashions, Style and Taste," *The Philosophy of Karl Popper*, ed. P. A. Schilpp (Open Court, 1974), vol. 2, 925–957. On Japanese aesthetics, see Yuriko Saito, *Everyday Aesthetics* (Oxford University Press, 2007). In "Fenomenología del Relajo," the Mexican philosopher Jorge Portilla analyzes the distinctive Mexican concept of "relajo" and discusses it in relation to irony, humor, laughter, and freedom. Portilla's essay is translated in Carlos Alberto Sánchez, *The Suspension of Seriousness: On the Phenomenology of Jorge Portilla* (SUNY Press, 2012).

5. Heather Widdows also summarizes the empirical evidence. See Heather Widdows, *Perfect Me: Beauty as an Ethical Ideal* (Princeton University Press, 2018). On Black aesthetics in the United States, see Paul C. Taylor, *Black Is Beautiful: A Philosophy of Black Aesthetics* (Wiley–Blackwell, 2016). An overview of ideas about the use of aesthetic life to maintain social injustice is Robin James, "Oppression, Privilege, and Aesthetics: The Use of the Aesthetic in Theories of Race, Gender, and Sexuality, and the Role of Race, Gender, and Sexuality in Philosophical Aesthetics," *Philosophy Compass* 8, no. 2 (2013): 101–116. A set of papers exploring aspects of the topic is Sherri Irvin, ed., *Body Aesthetics* (Oxford University Press, 2017). On aesthetic obligations and beauty ideals, see Alfred Archer and Lauren Ware, "Beyond the Call of Beauty: Everyday Aesthetic Demands Under Patriarchy," *Monist* 101, no. 1 (2018): 114–127. Sara Protasi argues that a loving gaze can counteract the beauty myth in

"The Perfect Bikini Body: Can We All Really Have It? Loving Gaze as an Antioppressive Beauty Ideal," *Thought* 6, no. 2 (2017): 93–101. A fascinating study of the aesthetic impact of mere exposure is James E. Cutting, "Gustave Caillebotte, French Impressionism, and Mere Exposure," *Psychonomic Bulletin and Review* 10 (2003): 319–343.

Index

*For the benefit of digital users, indexed terms that span two pages (e.g., 52–53)
may, on occasion, appear on only one of those pages.*

Tables and figures are indicated by *t* and *f* following the page number